MASTERING FEAR

Harness Emotion to Achieve Excellence in Health, Work, and Relationships

ROBERT MAURER, PhD

WITH MICHELLE GIFFORD, MA

CAREER
PRESS

The Career Press, Inc.
Wayne, NJ

MASTERING FEAR

EDITED BY ROGER SHEETY

TYPESET BY KRISTIN GOBLE

Cover design by Rob Johnson

Cover image by alexemanuel/iStock

Printed in the U.S.A.

To order this title, please call toll-free 1-800-CAREER-1 (NJ and Canada: 201-848-0310) to order using VISA or MasterCard, or for further information on books from Career Press.

The Career Press, Inc.

12 Parish Drive

Wayne, NJ 07470

www.careerpress.com

Library of Congress Cataloging-in-Publication Data

CIP Data Available Upon Request.

DEDICATION

For my friend, Steve Albert, whose courage, humor, passion, and compassion has inspired me to write this book and whose love and caring has given me strength and comfort.

ACKNOWLEDGMENTS

I am deeply grateful to the clients, the individuals, families, and organizations that have entrusted me with their confidence, reached to me for help, and given me the gift of contributing to their lives. Special thanks to my cowriter, Michelle Gifford, who has put words to my thoughts, added her wisdom and clarity, and who made this book possible. We are indebted to our agent, Sharon Bowers, who saw the potential of this material, and gave us support and guidance throughout this journey. For my wife Dia, and our cat Spot, who were both a source of energy and much needed distraction from the rigors of writing. To our publisher, Adam Grant, and our editor at Career Press, Kirsten Dalley, who have worked to bring this project to fruition and provided their insights and encouragement.

—Bob Maurer

For Mike and Jacob, who have steadfastly and with great heart supported every dream I've chosen to pursue—practical or not; and for Grandma, Aunt Karen, Connie, and my sisters, who have each provided me inspiration as this book came to life and who respond unfailingly every time I reach. With gratitude to Robert Maurer, my friend and mentor in this topic, who invited me to take part in this worthy adventure. In this time together, he has taught me more than he'll ever know and those I love.

—Michelle Gifford

CONTENTS

The Laws of Success

The success of humanity hinges on learning the laws of nature.

—Buckminster Fuller

We all strive for success. We work hard to achieve competence, recognition, and rewards in our work. We dream of finding the perfect mate and feeling the joy of giving and receiving love. We endeavor to eat right, exercise, and maintain good physical health. Yet for many of us, the success we yearn for remains elusive; and maintaining success seems impossible. Why do some people seem to have such a hard time succeeding in the three key areas of life: work, health, and relationships? And why do certain people achieve success only to destroy the very accomplishments they've worked so hard to attain?

These are questions I have struggled with for many years in my work as a business consultant and clinical psychologist. I've wondered why some very disciplined, successful people persistently fight weight gain, smoking, alcohol, and drugs; why individuals who desire romantic bliss repeatedly choose partners unsuitable for commitment and intimacy; and why stress disorders, which underlie so many other challenges, seem to be getting worse despite all of the research and experts out there to help.

Consider these all-too-familiar scenarios:

A hard-working, dedicated employee is promoted to a leadership position. He has trouble delegating and becomes increasingly ineffective, difficult to get along with, and aloof.

A romantic relationship begins with great optimism and excitement, then one partner becomes steadily more critical and distant, and finally disappears.

An individual achieves a dramatic improvement in health, changing lifelong patterns of drinking, smoking, or overeating; then a stressful event occurs and s/he resumes the habits so painstakingly changed.

Each person was devastated as their dreams slipped away.

As a professional working to help people at all stages and in all walks of life, situations like these confounded me for years and I wanted to know *why*. It seemed pointless to be helping people pursue and accomplish their life goals if I could not also help them master the skills necessary to sustain them once achieved.

But where would I look for the answers? Fortunately, the answers came looking for me. For most of my career to that point, I'd been doing what psychologists typically do: I worked with people who were struggling with some aspect of their lives, identifying the specific problems they faced and helping them to overcome those difficulties. This approach forever changed when I walked through the UCLA Medical School library one day and saw, sitting on a table, the book *Plagues and Peoples*[1] by William McNeill. The cover intrigued me, so I sat down and began to read. From that moment on, my professional life would never be the same. The book described how the whole course of human history has been radically influenced by diseases such as smallpox, malaria, and yellow fever. What fascinated me most, however, was not the illnesses themselves, nor even the devastation they caused. Instead, I was captivated by *how these plagues were cured*.

Prior to my visit to the library that day, I had assumed, as perhaps you do, that the way we remedy disease is by studying people who are ill and, from there, brilliant researchers in top-notch laboratories develop the miracle drugs needed for a cure. This is not, however, how the majority of these horrible maladies were tamed. Take smallpox for instance. This great killer had been around for thousands of years, taking the lives of an estimated 500 million people. Yet, the cure for this dreaded illness was not discovered through scientific experiments on the disease itself. Instead, it came about when someone began looking closely at who *wasn't* getting sick and then tried to figure out why.

In the midst of the smallpox epidemic in 18th century Britain, a country physician named Edward Jenner became intrigued by a common folktale claiming that milkmaids who had previously been sickened by cowpox would never get smallpox. Without knowing how the immune system works, Dr. Jenner developed a bold, creative experiment. He injected an 8-year-old boy first with the cowpox virus, then with a very small dose of smallpox. The boy developed resistance to the deadly disease and the use of this vaccination was thought to have saved more lives than any other invention in history.

Studying those who have stayed healthy in the presence of grave illness and discovering what was different about them has pointed the way to success in curing other diseases as well. Building the Panama Canal was perilous work, primarily due to the mosquito-borne infectious disease malaria. Many lives were spared, however, when an inquisitive physician by the name of Dr. William Crawford Gorgas began asking himself why the sailors aboard ships never became ill, whereas the people digging on land were so tragically susceptible. The difference, he cleverly surmised, was that the mosquitoes were drawn to the still water near the canal, whereas the sailors were steadily surrounded by ocean currents. Preventing this illness, he discovered, could be achieved by *replicating the environment of those who stayed well.*

As I read these accounts, I began to reflect on my own profession. Historically, the field of psychology had focused primarily on seeking accurate diagnoses—labels for people's problems—then designing effective treatments from there. After reading *Plagues and Peoples*, I began to believe that more significant breakthroughs could be made *not by observing those courageously struggling, but by looking at those who were succeeding and discovering what they were doing differently.* I concluded that, if psychology was to be most useful, our work should be focused on determining how successful people thrive. We should be replicating the conditions of those who are well.

With these thoughts in mind, I began searching worldwide for studies attempting to identify the *laws of success*—those skills necessary for people to succeed in all key areas of life: work, health, and relationships. Although I found many published books on success, I was discouraged to find that a vast majority focused on only one aspect of life: career success *or* relationship success *or* physical well-being. However, as I persisted in my research, I discovered many long-term studies that had followed large groups of people for years that attempted to discover what circumstances and skills are necessary to overcome adversity and sustain excellence across time. Among these investigations were the Kauai Longitudinal study,[2] the Terman Study of the Gifted,[3] the Harvard Grant Study,[4] and the Study of Adult Development (Glueck Study).[5] There is, of course, no straight line to success and no one can achieve and hold onto success without some setbacks along the way. However, each of these investigations contributed meaningful insights regarding the fundamental principles or the *"laws" of success.*

The Kauai Longitudinal study followed 698 infants born on the island in 1955. They were followed from the time they were in the womb through the next 40 years. The Hawaiian Islands are a researcher's paradise, as many inhabitants live on the same island and utilize the same limited social, health, and educational resources throughout their lifetime, which makes tracking information across time relatively easy. As the study progressed, the principle investigator, Dr. Emmy Werner, began to take a special interest in a particular subset of this population. These were "high-risk" children who, despite exposure to stress during pregnancy, premature birth, discordant and impoverished home lives, and uneducated, alcoholic, and/or mentally disturbed parents, went on to develop healthy personalities, stable careers, and strong interpersonal relationships. One out of three of these high-risk children "grew into competent young adults who loved well, worked well, and played well. None developed serious learning or behavioral problems in childhood or adolescence." Dr. Werner and her team studied this group to identify the protective factors that contributed to the resilience of these children.

The Terman Study of the Gifted followed 1528 children in California schools who were labeled gifted both by teachers and as a result of intelligence tests. These children were born between 1900 and 1925, were predominantly white, and most were from middle and upper-class families—a population born with every advantage. The study began in the 1920s and some individuals are still studied to this day. The question was, was it superior intellect or some other set of skills that allowed some of these people to live happy, healthy lives whereas others struggled?

The Harvard Grant Study was a 75-year observation of the lives of 268 male Harvard sophomores from varied backgrounds—some privileged, some not—who attended college between 1939 and 1944. They have since been interviewed and given physical exams every two years. During the same period of time, the Study of Adult Development (also called the Glueck Study) was initiated by Harvard Researchers. This study, which continues today, followed the lives of 465 low-income children born in the Boston area between 1940 and 1945.

Through very different ages and stages of life, each of these investigations sought to identify the laws of success—those critical skills that allowed individuals to attain and sustain excellence in their work, health, *and* relationships across time. What was surprising was the high degree of similarity in the conclusions they reached, despite the very different populations studied. In the pages that follow, we will explore the surprising research that points to the fact that there is, indeed, a "fork in the road," a critical turning point that promotes or prevents success based on how individuals perceive stress and how they choose to respond to fear; and we will reveal the one skill essential for achieving and sustaining success in our work, health, and relationships.

Happy families are all alike, but each unhappy family is unhappy in its own way.
—Leo Tolstoy (*Anna Karenina*)

One can have no smaller or greater mastery than mastery of oneself.
—Leonardo da Vinci

CHAPTER 1

The Biology of Fear

There is No Such Thing as Stress

According to recent surveys, stress is a challenge for most of us. An American Psychological study in 2007 found that close to one-third of all survey respondents described their stress as "extreme" and nearly half felt that their stress was getting worse. Stress is considered a primary underlying factor in many health problems, relationship tensions, and lost productivity at work. Knowing this, it might seem strange to you—even outlandish—for me to tell you that: *There is no such thing as stress. Stress, as we know it, does not exist!*

In fact, what we are currently calling stress may be something else entirely and I hope to convince you that stress would be best addressed by a different name. To begin our journey, consider the findings of one recent study on stress. A group of researchers followed 30,000 subjects for eight years examining the relationship among reported levels of stress, perceptions of stress, and mortality outcomes.[1] At the beginning of the study, investigators asked people to rate their levels of stress. Then, eight years later, they examined public records to see whether or not the reported levels of stress could predict who would still be alive. At first glance, the results seemed exactly what we might predict. Those subjects who had indicated that their stress levels were high at the beginning of the study were 43 percent more likely to have died during the eight subsequent years. However, the findings turned out to be more complicated than that. At the onset of the study, researchers had asked not only how extreme the person felt their stress level was, but also whether or not the person felt that the stress was harmful to their health. It turned out that only the subjects who *feared that the stress was harmful* suffered its ill effects. The investigators scrupulously ruled out other possible causes for this dramatic finding, leaving us asking: "What's happening here?"

With that question in mind, let's begin by exploring a bit of "stress" history. Do you know how old the concept of stress is? It's a little known fact that "stress" sat around in the science of metallurgy (the contortion of metals) for 500 years bothering no one until the early 20th century when it became a medical disorder that no one has been able to cure. Since its discovery, humankind has cured polio and tuberculosis and has made strides with virtually every form of cancer. Physicians, psychologists, spiritual advisors, and others have been working diligently to identify, describe, and attempt to cure this modern "disease." But, despite the extensive research, thousands of experts, and multitude of books and articles on the topic, very little progress has been made.

The Biology of Fear

The lion, the gazelle, the monkey, and me; we all have something in common that profoundly affects the success we achieve—or don't—in life.

So why haven't we been able to cure stress? The answer lies in the design of the brain. The human brain has been given two essential tasks: regulating the body and surviving in the world. Every other activity is a luxury. The bottom layer is our brainstem, often called the "reptilian brain." This portion looks like the full brain of an alligator and it's responsible for most of our basic bodily functions, such as reminding our hearts to beat and our lungs to take in air. This is what keeps us alive when the two other layers are damaged, as when someone is in a coma. The top, or outer layer, is the cortex. This is our luxury—the part that makes us most human. Wrapped around the midbrain, the cortex is where consciousness, problem-solving, and creativity live. Sitting unobtrusively between these two layers lies the powerful midbrain, home to our emotions and key to our survival. The midbrain is often called "the mammalian brain," because we share the design with all other mammals, most similarly the chimpanzee.

The task of survival is assigned to the amygdala, an exquisite little almond-shaped structure located in the bottom portion of the midbrain. This structure governs the body's primitive "fight or flight" response, and is responsible for four Fs in life:

food (appetite regulation), *fight, flight,* and sex (yep, you guessed it—*fornication*). The fight or flight response is the highly effective alarm system that prepares the body for action. To get a feel for this extraordinary system, just imagine yourself as a lion, lying peacefully in the African savannah enjoying the warm sunshine. You open one lazy eye and spot a delicious gazelle grazing 50 yards away. Your eye sends the message to your amygdala, which rapidly dispatches the information necessary to prepare your body to pursue this new opportunity—lunch has arrived! The gazelle, pausing between bites, sees you lift your head. Its eyes send your threatening image to its amygdala, which immediately prepares it to escape the misfortune about to befall.

Whether running toward opportunity or away from danger, the amygdala triggers the exact same set of bodily responses—both animals become equally primed for action. Pupils dilate to let in more information and the heart races, speeding up circulation of blood to the muscles. The muscles of the upper neck and lower back are tensed, preparing the legs for action. The mouth becomes dry, the stomach slams shut, and appetite is lost. If two gazelle are mating and they sense a lion charging, do you think one of them turns to the other and says, "Wadda you think sweetheart, is it worth it?" Of course not! The blood supply immediately leaves the genitals, preparing the animal for flight. The animals get rid of excess baggage (waste products) so they can run faster and explosive diarrhea and urination ensue. The quintessential example, some might suggest, of being "scared shitless and pissed off!"

All mammals, including humans, possess this primitive, highly effective alarm system that prepares the body in response to opportunity (the lion) or threat (the gazelle). *It is the most life-saving mechanism in the brain.* But let's take a minute now to consider the symptoms: racing heart, dry mouth, shortness of breath, neck, back, and stomach pain, frequent urination, diarrhea, change in appetite, headache, insomnia, and loss of libido. Does the list sound familiar? I expect it does. If you look up the symptoms of stress or anxiety in any medical textbook, you'll find that the "disease" symptoms listed are *identical to any body's healthy, natural response to fear.* When the body's alarm system—its fight or flight response—is switched on for hours, days, or weeks at a time, it creates a sense of "dis-ease" in the body. The result is what we now call a *stress disorder.* The term *stress* is humankind's attempt to take one of nature's finest gifts to our bodies and label it a disease!

So what difference does it make if we call this alarm system *stress* or *fear?* More than you might imagine. To understand how a simple choice of words can affect our long-term success in all areas of life, let's begin first by looking at a fundamental problem with our current use of the word stress. The father of stress research, Dr. Hans Seyle first coined the term in 1938, making a clear distinction between a "stress response" and "stress" itself. He identified life challenges—our jobs, the traffic, financial struggles, relationship trials—as *stressors* and the body's inability to deal successfully with these challenges as *stress.*

Stressors are external threats or challenges.

Stress is our body's reaction to those challenges.

In today's world, we have confused our stressors with stress, and we now erroneously believe that the source of the problem is the mortgage, the difficult marriage, the unruly children, the demanding boss, the unfinished projects (threats), or even the recent promotion, the new house, or the budding relationship (opportunities). People rarely have control over their stressors, yet most of us persist in attempting to "cure" stress by endeavoring to control them. People unsuccessfully blame external factors—life situations and other people—for their chronic discomfort and high-alert state (*stress disorder*), rather than seeking to address the body's unhealthy, often changeable, *stress response*. Incorrectly identifying the *source* of the problem leads people to make excuses rather than progress.

The Vocabulary of Fear

Many of us today use words like "stress, anxiety, depression," or "nerves" to describe a strong, persistent feeling of upset in our bodies. However, throughout my research, I have been especially intrigued by how rarely highly successful people use these words to describe the uncomfortable feelings typically associated with stress. As I watched interview after interview of incredibly successful people talking about their lives, I noticed that they consistently used different words to capture this experience. They all used the word *fear* or one of its synonyms (afraid, scared, etc.) to describe the physiological responses we all share.

At first, it seemed a simple matter of semantics, possibly not worth further investigation. However, after a while, the frequency of so many successful people using the words "fear" or "scared" was hard to ignore. For example, consider the book *Creativity*,

Inc.[2] by Ed Catmull, president of the hugely successful film production company Pixar. The story of the history, evolution, and processes used by this magical studio—creator of epic animated movies such as *Toy Story, Finding Nemo,* and *Monsters, Inc.*—is inspiring to read. Most interesting to me, however, was the fact that in the book Catmull used the word "anxiety" once and "stress" once, but used "fear" or "scared" *78 times!* "If we aren't always at least a little *scared,*" he wrote, "we are not doing our job."[3]

Ed Catmull is not the only highly successful person who chooses to use these powerful words regularly. Note how many others who have achieved remarkable results in the world have used the words *fear* or its synonyms:

> *When you are running an institution, you are always* **scared** *at first. You are* **afraid** *you'll break it. People don't think about leaders this way but it is true. Everyone who is running something goes home at night and wrestles with the same* **fear***. Am I going to be the one who blows this place up?*
>
> —Jack Welch, past-CEO, General Electric

> *All adventures, especially into new territory, are* **scary***.*
>
> —Sally Ride, astronaut

> *Never let the* **fear** *of striking out get in your way.*
>
> —Babe Ruth, baseball player

> **Fear** *is your ally. The minute you come onto a set and you're no longer* **afraid***, you are in big trouble.*
>
> —Stephen Spielberg, author and producer

*I'm coming from a place of acting, so you're never quite sure if you're going to get the crew to even be on your side and you always have this great **fear** that they will discover that you're an imposter and that you have no business being there.*

—George Clooney, actor (*Los Angeles Times*, January 27, 2012)

*You gain strength, courage, and confidence by each experience in which you really stop to look **fear** in the face. You are able to say to yourself, "I have lived through this horror. I can take the next thing to come along."*

—Eleanor Roosevelt, First Lady

*If you can take the time to understand **fear**, you can use it. I was always a little **afraid** in each game I played. **Afraid** of failure, of letting my teammates down, and of being hurt. I used that **fear** to make me a better player.*

—Lynn Swanson, NFL player on four Super Bowl teams

I was puzzled. Why would so many successful people prefer the word *fear* over *stress?* Then one day, while I was following one of our resident physicians through her clinic visits, the answer suddenly became obvious. As an educator on faculty at two medical schools, through the past 25 years it has been my responsibility to help students in family medicine excel in their communication with patients and families. In this role, I spend more than half of my time shadowing new doctors on their rounds, observing their interactions, and providing feedback about their clinical work and bedside manner. As a result, I've witnessed thousands of interactions with patients and family members as they've faced surgery, pregnancy, diabetes, cancer, rashes, insomnia, heart disease, aging, and more. While listening to patients that day, I began to recognize the very different vocabularies used by adults and children when describing feelings of "upset" or emotional pain in their bodies. When adults talk with a doctor, they almost always used words such as *depressed, anxious, stressed, nervous,* or *tense.* But children never use these words. They talk about being *scared or afraid.*

Tell me, have you ever heard a child say she was "anxious" about the boogey man? Or he was "depressed" because the other kids at school were going to the zoo, but he was going to the hospital for surgery? Of course not! Children state things simply and directly—they are *scared, mad, sad.* At some point, you have probably witnessed another adult crying who immediately reached for a tissue and apologized, saying something like, "Oh, I'm so sorry. You must think I'm such a weakling!" Children, on the other hand, cry freely, sobbing loudly with snot dripping down their faces, not apologizing for a thing. So why do children simply cut to the chase? It's because children know they live in a world that they cannot control. They can't control whether their parents are in a good mood or bad or whether their new teacher will be nice or mean. They can't control thunder and lightning, the stomach flu, or who will be their best friend at recess tomorrow. As a result, children seem to have a different relationship than adults do with emotional joy and pain.

Give this a try. Sit down with a young child; ask him what he wants for Christmas and you're in for a 20-minute discussion. Then, ask what he's afraid of—another 20-minute conversation will definitely ensue. What kind of movies do kids love to stand in line to see? Scary ones! Children accept that they live in a world of fear, so they figure that they might as well have some fun and learn to deal with it in the process. Because they lack control over so many aspects of their world, and because they accept this lack of control, children can easily discuss their fears.

By the time we become adults, however, fear is no longer seen by most of us as a normal, healthy part of life, but instead something we get angry at for showing up. In a culture obsessed with self-reliance and the preservation of self-esteem, the term *fear* has become a four-letter word. We do not accept our lack of control and so we rarely learn how to deal with it successfully. We consider fear a disease. We call it stress and blame the person or situation that triggered the feeling rather than addressing the fear itself. Let me see if I can convince you of this in two ways:

First, right now, put down your book and call up a friend. Wait for a natural pause in the conversation, then ask, "So, what are you afraid of?" Do you think this will trigger an interesting conversation or will your friend question your sanity and change the topic? Probably the latter. It's a question that makes most people uncomfortable. As mentioned earlier, most of us have banished fear from our conversations and awareness, focusing instead on the external problems we face while labeling the body's most powerful and basic emotion a disease.

A second exercise demonstrating our strange, unmindful relationship with fear is one I use with audiences all over the world. I begin by saying, "Please raise your hand if you are afraid to cross the street." In a room of 100 people, one or two hesitant hands will lift. *Okay.* I then say, "So, if I were to blindfold you and ask you to cross the street, would you then be afraid?" All hands go up. *Good—we're making progress.* "One final question. Imagine you and I are walking down the street, engrossed in conversation. You sense that we're getting close to a busy crossing, but I appear to be oblivious to the rapidly passing cars. As we reach the intersection, do you keep eye contact with me as we cross the street? Of course not! No matter how rude it might seem, you'll break eye contact, look left and right, and assure that the cars have stopped before crossing." I pause for some reflection time, then conclude: "We engage in this elaborate set of behaviors for only one reason—we are *afraid* that if we don't, the results will be painful. For this reason, I suggest that we are *all* afraid to cross the street."

What these exercises convey to us is that *fear is a gift.* But most of us have forgotten that, just as we've forgotten that we're afraid to cross the street. When we visit cities like New York, London, or Rome, where the rules between cars and pedestrians may be different than what we're familiar with, we need to adapt in order to survive. So, at these times, we become more aware of our fear. Where do you think we are most likely to get hit by a car—in a crosswalk or jaywalking? We are *four times* more likely to get hit in a crosswalk! Because when we're jaywalking, we know that we're not where we're supposed to be, so we think much more about the car danger and potential police officers, and the street has our complete attention. But in a crosswalk, there is an illusion of safety. And there, metaphorically speaking, is where most of us spend our lives.

Now, it's not likely that forgetting you are afraid to cross the street will get you into any real trouble—your parents did too good of a job training you. The important point to consider is that if you have forgotten that fear, are there any other fears you have buried along the way?

If I'd asked you before reading this chapter if you'd like to live your life fearlessly, many of you would have leapt at the offer. Everyone has a long list of times when we believe that fear has gotten in our way. I hope that by now, however, you will consider the possibility that fear is a gift. Without it, you might not live another week! Consider the many simple behaviors we engage in out of fear every day:

- Do you wear your seatbelt when you get into the car? If so, is it due to the sheer pleasure of having that strip of cloth across your chest? Of course not! You're either afraid of going through the windshield or of getting a ticket.
- Do you take better care of your teeth the week before you go to the dentist? Is this because your teeth and gums are in greater need than they are the other 51 weeks of the year?
- Do you make some food choices based on what is best for your body rather than what might taste best, or exercise with the thought that your body might not otherwise sustain you as you age?

I hope that by now we all agree that everyone experiences fear at some level on a daily basis. So, you might ask, what does this have to do with achieving success? To answer this question, let me share the *first law of success*—the first half of the one essential skill for creating and maintaining excellence in health, career, and relationships. It is to do what successful people do—develop *an awareness and acceptance of fear.* Successful people are consistently aware and accepting of their fears. They assume that whenever they are doing something important, fear will show. The bigger the streets they want to cross, metaphorically speaking (for example, creating a loving relationship, dealing with a promotion, starting a new business, or committing to a healthy lifestyle), the more fear will be present.

If you want to improve your skills in becoming more aware and accepting of fear, I recommend that you consider reading Susan Jeffers' book, *Feel the Fear and Do It Anyway*[4] to glean her insightful perspectives on the subject. You may also want to try out the following two exercises:

First, sit across the table from another adult and begin a conversation. Start by having one person ask, "What are you afraid of?" and the other partner respond each time with, *"I'm afraid . . ."* or *"I'm scared. . . ."* Fill in the blank with any fear large or small that you can remember, anticipate, or imagine. You might begin by saying, "I am afraid to do this exercise." Go back and forth with your partner for five minutes, taking turns asking and answering the question. As you proceed with this exercise, remember that you don't need to be profound. Most fears are genuinely simple and very childlike.

At least once each day, when you or someone else is upset, assume that there is an underlying fear and try to discover what it might be.

Do all upsets come from fear? We don't know for sure. However, based on the research, I suggest that this is a most useful way of looking at them. The spiritual literature suggests that there are just two basic human fears: *a fear of not being worthwhile,* which tends to be associated with self-esteem (for example: Why didn't I get that promotion? Why don't my friends call me back? Why can't I find love? What if my new venture doesn't succeed?) and a *fear of losing control,* which we tend to associate with health or financial concerns. Let me demonstrate how broadly you can apply fear to any upset. Do you or does anyone you know get frustrated in traffic? If I were to suggest to you that the only reason we get upset in traffic is because we're afraid, would that sound ridiculous? Consider this scenario:

You woke up this morning because the alarm clock triggered your amygdala. If you are highly spiritually evolved, your first thought was: "Thank God I get to live another day!" For those of us not so spiritually advanced, however, those first thoughts may have a slightly different ring. They may sound something more like this: "You should have gone to bed earlier! You shouldn't have had that cake last night!

You should have gotten up an hour ago to exercise! You have way too much to do today—get out of bed!"

Does this harsh voice, or some version of it, sound somewhat familiar? For many of us, these are the words that greet us with the miracle of life each morning. A host of underlying fears, all of them rushing in to help us start our day.

Now imagine that I greeted you by saying, "How was your shower this morning?" You would think I was crazy! And yet, the shower is one of the most sensual parts of our day. The miracle of that warm, clean water pouring over our pain-free bodies—some days, that's as good as life gets! But what are most of us typically doing in the shower? Oblivious to the pleasure of the moment and the boost to our physical health, we are busy building our list of what we need to accomplish (or what we can't accomplish) that day. We rehearse our schedule and plans and potential failures until we're out the door and, by the time we reach the roadway, all those cars are standing between us and our list! When we get to work, we're feeling rushed and behind-schedule. Excited about last night's big game, a friend stops to ask if we saw it. We make the mistake of saying "no" and he takes this as an invitation to tell us all about it, play by play. By the end of his story, we're seething—this fool standing between us and our list! And that list is standing between us and our feelings of *self-worth, self-esteem, and accomplishment.* Do you see now how fear may underlie even the simplest upsets in life: a late shower, cars on the highway, a talkative colleague, or any other frustration?

You may want to consider keeping a journal of these sorts of observations for a time, to help establish the habit of looking for and becoming more aware of underlying fears. As you explore this idea, remember that we suggest that most fears can be reduced to either a fear of losing control (usually referring to health or finance) or a fear of not being worthwhile. To help you get started, here are a few examples of "upsets"—anger, frustration, irritation—that may develop from an underlying fear:

- "I'm upset with my friend for not returning my call." *I may not be valuable enough to that friend, proof that I am not worthwhile or important.*
- "I'm upset with my spouse for not doing more around the house." *If he or she loved me more, they would treat my needs more seriously; or, if I had more help, I would feel less out of control.*
- "I'm upset with a colleague at work who is taking all the credit for a collaborative project." *I'm afraid if they start laying people off, I may be seen as less valuable and could lose my job; or, I'm afraid my colleague sees me as weak and thinks I can be trampled on in this way.*
- "I'm upset with all the people who take advantage of me!" *I am afraid to say no and risk other people's rejection. Doing for others gives me a sense of importance. I'm afraid if I stop doing for others, I'll feel worthless.*

It's important that we don't confuse our desire to recognize and address our fears with a wish to eliminate them entirely. For most of our existence as a species on this planet, we've lived as hunters and gatherers. We did not see as well, run as fast, or have the strength of the animals who preyed upon us. When we came out of our caves, it was useful—essential really—that we approach the world with caution (another grown-up word for fear). What I am suggesting to you, then, is that fear can be a guide and a friend and it remains as essential for our survival and success in today's world as it was in the wild.

Recognizing our underlying fears, however, helps us to quiet the amygdala and allows us to more easily identify specific ways in which we might address a challenge. In later chapters we will address the fact that denying fear's existence or getting angry when you encounter fear can lead to anxiety or depression. This can defeat the value of fear in guiding us to confront and resolve the challenges of life. When these same fears are recognized and addressed in constructive ways, people's lives tend to flourish.

A study in the *American Journal of Psychiatry* dramatically illustrates the danger of not having a typical fear response in today's world. A group of 400 children was assessed at age three to identify environmental risk factors such as lack of parental education, poverty, and being born to teenage parents. Additionally, each was assessed to determine their fear response. Twenty years later, these same children (now young adults) were evaluated to determine which of them had been convicted of serious crimes.[5] The best predictor for the likelihood of criminal convictions in adulthood was the person's lack of fear response at age three. The authors of the study hypothesized that a poorly functioning amygdala led to a weak fear response. This finding aligns with similar studies, which have found that psychopaths have a poorly functioning amygdala as well. So you see, as uncomfortable as it may feel at times, fear is good for human beings and it is essential to our well-being!

I suspect that, by now, you're beginning to wonder what all this information about fear has to do with success? Successful people find fear as uncomfortable as anyone else does, however instead of rejecting or avoiding it, they see it as a signal that something important is happening that requires their attention. As children do, they assume that fear is a natural part of life, and they know that whenever they're doing something important, fear will show up. Fear is something to be recognized, embraced, and boldly addressed; and developing an acceptance and awareness of fear is crucial in maintaining success in work, health, and relationships.

In today's world, what we currently call stress often hampers our happiness and stalls our success in many areas of life. And yet, with all of our collective efforts, we have not yet been able to cure it. Why is this? As we mentioned earlier, the primary reason is because there is no such thing as stress. Stress is actually *fear* trapped in a culture with an unhealthy relationship to that emotion. The "stress symptoms" listed at the beginning of this chapter are not signs of disease. They are our body's gift to us to let us know something important is happening that requires our immediate attention. Without these symptoms we would have perished as a species long ago.

We do not want to be afraid of fear. Recall the study mentioned earlier in this chapter where, of 30,000 adults who reported high levels of stress, only those who believed that stress was harmful met an early death. "Stress" was not the villain—*it was the fear that stress was harmful* that was the danger.

Fear is designed to help and protect us and it gives us the tools to solve life's challenges if we use it well. As Kelly McGonigal writes in *The Upside of Stress*: "The energy you get from stress doesn't just help your body act; it also fires up your brain. Adrenaline wakes up your senses. Your pupils dilate to let in more light and your hearing sharpens. The brain processes what you perceive more quickly. Mind wandering stops and less important priorities drop away. Stress can create a state of concentrated attention, one that gives you access to more information about your physical environment."[6] Remember the responses of the lion and gazelle? What McGonigal is describing here is the upside of *fear*.

So, if we wish to alleviate stress and improve our chances of success in all areas of life, then the question becomes: "Just what *is* a human being's healthy response to fear?" Let's travel forward into the next chapter to unearth the answers.

CHAPTER 2

What Not to Do
With Fear

Courage is resistance to fear, mastery of fear, not the
absence of fear.

—Mark Twain

Animals in the wild follow the laws of nature. Each has a built-in
response to fear that increases their chance of survival and quiets
the fear response. When a lion is afraid, it attacks. When a bird
hears a twig snap, it flies to a higher branch. When a deer smells a
foreign scent from one direction, it runs the opposite way. When
a mouse is afraid, it burrows in its hole. If it makes it there in
time, the amygdala quiets and the fear mechanism shuts off. If a

hawk eats it, the response ceases as well. Each animal has a pre-scribed, hard-wired response that leads to a cessation of fear and, hopefully, success. The animal moves and, once danger or oppor-tunity has passed (usually in a matter of seconds or minutes), it relaxes and goes back to what it was doing before. Although they differ in the life-saving actions they take, all mammals possess this instinctive system, which is designed to respond to brief, sud-den threats in the environment. It leads to quick action and sur-vival—or not—and it can be activated and de-activated a hundred times a day at no cost to the animal's health.

Human beings share this automatic, life-saving response with other mammals. Urgent threats ("stressors") are the kinds that our bodies were originally designed to respond to as well. However, these are not the common stressors for most people today. Unlike animals in the wild, many of our threats are not immediate. They persist, at least in our minds, across long periods of time. This is what defines a "stress disorder." It is the alarm system of the body staying on for days or weeks at a time, causing wear, tear, and damage to those vulnerable parts of the body that participate in the fight or flight response. In all of the animal kingdom, human beings are the only mammals to acquire stress disorders—with the exception of the animals we have domesticated. Dogs and cats have been hanging around with us for thousands of years and so they, too, now share many of our bad habits.

In the last chapter, we identified some of the physiological symptoms associated with fear that are now typically called "stress symptoms." These included responses such as rapid heart rate, loss of appetite, and tensed muscles. When the amygdala is pressed to function for longer, sustained periods of time, additional symptoms and warning signs emerge that are not always as easy to feel. These include things such as increased heart rate (leading to high blood pressure), digestive tract dysfunction (leading to nausea and pain), lowered immune function (making us better hosts for germs and viruses), loss of libido (sex hormones are suppressed), and altered brain function, which results in loss of creativity, memory problems, trouble concentrating, impaired judgment, and poor impulse control, just to name a few. Tragically, the exquisite alarm system that was designed to alert us to danger and help us quickly take action to protect ourselves now seems to be making many of us ill. So the critical question is: "Just how do we turn the alarm system off?"

It is highly unlikely that our maker left just one species to make up its own rule for the most life-saving emotion of the brain. Take a moment right now to see if you can answer this question for yourself: if the lion charges, the bird flies, and the mouse burrows in response to fear, just what is it that *we* are supposed to do when we are afraid?

Before I convince you that the human brain does, indeed, have its own law for what it wants us to do when we are afraid and, if we obey this law, we maximize our chances for good physical health and sustained career and relationship success, I want to briefly share some of the more common, although unfortunate, ways that people respond to persistent fear. Because few of us are taught how to respond to fear in a positive, healthy way, many of us are "afraid of fear" and will do anything to avoid the feeling. Almost always, what we do to circumvent fear creates more and bigger problems. Following are seven frequently used strategies that *do not work* in response to fear. In fact, these tend to make fear, the stress response, and most situations much worse. To help you easily recall the list, let's use the mnemonic: "DANGERS."

Depression

Anger

Negotiation

Griping

Eating

Rumination

Substances

The **D** stands for **Depression**. Although there is much about depression that remains a mystery, there is some evidence supporting the idea that depression may be one result of long-term activation of the amygdala; and certain mild depression may mask underlying fear. For example, a person who has been looking for a job unsuccessfully for nine months might be afraid of repeated rejection and/or the financial hardship. In this case, depression may provide a balm, or mask, for these fears. A single person interested in dating may tell a friend that Internet dating and bars are "depressing," when, in fact, those situations actually scare him. In this case, depression may seem less painful than the fear of rejection. In these cases, people are said to be "depressing" their fears. In the clinical setting, I have often observed that when patients' depression starts to lift through counseling or medication, they become uncomfortable with the underlying fears (usually referred to as "anxieties") that begin to surface as they gain energy and begin moving toward their goals. Whether depression is the result of the short or long-term activation of the amygdala it may be masking important fears that need to be addressed.

The **A** represents Anger. Although not a disease in itself, anger is very hard on the heart. Anger as a response to fear is not only common, but often appears socially acceptable. For example, imagine you are at a party and your sweetheart is having a lot of fun with someone else. I mean *a lot of fun*. Is it likely that you would approach her and gently say, "You seem to be having a lot of fun with this good-looking guy and I'm just a little bit afraid"? Or, are you more likely to say, "I hate these parties, your friends are boring—all they talk about is work—and the food stinks. Let's go!"? For many people, anger is the easiest response to fear. However, it is a destructive response that, once again, does not address and quiet underlying fears. If you think that getting angry may be a helpful response to fear, let me recommend a book for you: *Anger Kills*[1] by cardiologist Dr. Redford Williams. In his book, Dr. Williams clearly demonstrates how anger can dramatically increase the risks of heart disease and death. He also provides a scientifically valid test to assess whether or not you evidence the behavior of turning fear into anger. If you find that you lean toward an anger response to fear, you may also want to consider reviewing the excellent strategies he suggests for addressing this risk.

The **N** stands for Negotiation. Negotiation seems to have much to recommend it. It is the act of cooperation and compromise.

However, when people attempt to negotiate without an aware-ness of fear, it can lead to trouble. In one of the best-selling books on negotiation, *Getting to Yes* by Roger Fisher and William Ury, they repeatedly remind the reader that "the reason we negotiate is because we can't give the other party what they want."[2] If you could, you would call it Christmas! I stopped counting after the 27th time they used the phrase "fear" or "concern" in the book. The authors suggest that, in order to achieve a successful nego-tiation, it is first necessary to identify the other party's fear, and then find a way to address the fear that the other person has not considered. Although that is an ideal approach in theory, unfor-tunately many of us begin to negotiate without ever being aware of others' fears, or even acknowledging our own!

To get a better sense of how negotiating without an awareness of fear might increase, rather than decrease, the stress response, let me share a personal example that a UCLA family medicine resident and her husband recently shared with me. This woman had been a resident for about six months, with a very challenging work schedule. Her husband was a graduate student on campus with a schedule no easier than hers. They woke up one week-end morning with that familiar exhaustion that occurs when the work week takes too much out of you. They were sitting together in a local restaurant eating breakfast in complete silence. He was watching the top of her head as she ate and was becoming more and more frightened, thinking, "Is this it? Is this all we're going to have for the rest of our lives? Have we sacrificed our intimacy and our marriage on this alter of success?" But instead of voicing this fear, he did what most of us would do—he shared a possible solution to it. He broke the silence enthusiastically, saying: "When we graduate, let's head off to Europe. We'll travel the world together. It'll be wonderful!" His wife, having no idea that this conversation had anything to do with fear, thought he was talking about travel and she responded in accord with her own underlying fears: "That sounds like so much trouble! Passports, luggage, visas. When I graduate, I just want to sit on the beach and do nothing." Hearing the solution to his fears dashed, and hearing her say "I" instead of "we" (which greatly increased those fears), he became annoyed. She sensed his annoyance and, not understanding it, got angry, saying, "What are you getting upset about?! We're talking about something two and a half years from now! Don't we have enough to worry about now without you looking for new problems?!" We all know what it's like when we're tired—any irritation is like a match to fumes. Especially at those times, negotiating without an awareness of fear—our own or others'—can result in alerting the amygdala more rather than calming it. This can cause additional problems in relationships in any setting.

The **G** stands for Griping. We may see this response to fear frequently in any relationship or organization undergoing big changes. Individuals can become very negative, complaining loudly and in-depth as they struggle with uncertainty (another "grown-up" word for fear) in the workplace, community, at home, or even in their own bodies as they age or as health concerns arise. Major upheavals such as reorganizations or layoffs, changing technology, changes in family membership or dynamics, and critical illness may all trigger this ineffective response to fear. Griping can temporarily mask fears and calm the amygdala by tricking the mind into believing that you are reaching out and calling for a solution. However, when griping becomes persistent, it frequently serves to increase our fears and those of others. When it becomes redundant, griping can lead to verbal rumination—rehearsing the threat—yet another ineffective response to addressing our fears.

The E stands for Eating. Did you know that it is physically impossible for a person to eat and be afraid at the same time? As we described in Chapter 2, the ancient amygdala was designed to respond to immediate, life-challenging threats. It shuts down appetite when danger or opportunity approaches to assure that we attack or escape rather than continuing to eat! Conversely, the moment we put food on our tongues, the amygdala assumes the threat has gone away. It shuts off in an instant and our fears are gone. The problem with addressing our fears in this way is that, the moment an anxious person swallows the cookie or potato chip and goes back to worrying, the amygdala turns right back on, requiring more food to quiet it once again. For this reason, eating is not only an ineffective way to address our fears, it can become exceptionally dangerous to our health.

The R stands for Rumination or "worry." Instead of facing their fears directly, many people will persist in mentally rehearsing, again and again, all the ways they might get hurt or fail. Yet, they don't take action to address these fears. Worry can be a healthy emotion, but only if it leads to a protective action. You worry before crossing the street, so you look both ways. You worry about being late to the airport and missing your flight, so you leave a bit early. You worry about getting the measles or flu, so you get a vaccination. These worries assist you in adapting your behavior so you will succeed in being safe and achieving your goals. On the other hand, worrying about a test but not studying any harder, or worrying if you will ever meet the right person while staying home and hiding, are clearly not helpful. Rumination is worry without resolution. It typically it leads to an escalation of the fight or flight response rather than calming our fears.

The **S** represents Substances. Drugs such as alcohol, nicotine, marijuana, and other street or misused prescription drugs may appear to provide a rapid, effective means of calming immediate or persistent fears. Although they may seem to work in the moment, the long-term consequences for individuals are enormous, and they usually come at a colossal cost to those nearby as well. Using drugs or alcohol to calm fears is a dangerous strategy. Abusing substances of any kind can lead to depression, disruption in the capacity to work, inability to maintain personal and professional relationships, and increased risk of illness or even death. However, clinical efforts to help people avoid using substances by doing things that upset them often backfire. When smokers, for example, were shown either frightening footage of a smoke-charred lung during an autopsy or a patient dying of lung cancer in the hospital, they often became so upset that they left the room and then smoked to reduce their fear! For this reason, people struggling with substance use are usually most successful when their underlying fears are addressed first.[3]

Consider Alex, a past patient of mine who used substances as a primary means of addressing his fears. I met Alex when he was 28. At 17, Alex looked to all the world to be an exemplary teenager. His grades were exceptional, he was an accomplished athlete on the soccer team, and he appeared to his friends to have an enviable life. But Alex felt enormous pressure to succeed. Each A in class, each star performance on the athletic field, each word of praise felt like an additional brick of pressure. He described it in this way: "I was always thinking, 'How can I keep this up . . . and what happens when I fail?'" Eventually, the way Alex chose to cope with his daily fear of failure, his fear of falling short of perfection, was to use and abuse substances. He confided in no one and was isolated from his family and friends. Even in the safety of a psychologist's office many years later, Alex found it extremely painful to share his self-doubts.

After his second DWI, Alex's parents (much against his wishes) admitted him to a substance-abuse treatment program. At first he battled the counselors, but eventually he applied his determination to be successful to the goal of sobriety. After four months of inpatient treatment, Alex returned to school and his family. As hard as it had been for him to become sober, and as great a triumph he had achieved over his addiction, he found that he returned to all the pressures he had felt before. His self-doubt and inner demand for perfection, along with his fear of failure, were waiting for him like a puppy outside the door of his home. When the fears became too great, he relapsed and alcohol and drugs once again became his primary companions.

Alex's challenges were typical of those any addict might face. A person struggles with alcohol or drug use, finds the courage to achieve sobriety, and then a life crisis or persistent challenge sends them back to that substance to calm their fears. When Alex arrived in my office, our task in counseling was not to get him sober one more time. He knew how to do that without my help. Our goal was to help him face his fears and find healthier ways to address them. The take home point here is that alcohol and drug use at any level does not shut off the amygdala in the long-term. Like eating, every time the substance fades, the fear returns in greater force. Substance use and abuse is a short-term solution that doesn't address the underlying need. Not addressing the fear is not only one of the primary contributors to relapse, but to developing a problem in the first place.

So now we are all familiar with seven common, unhealthy responses to the life-saving gift of fear: Depression, Anger, Negotiation, Griping, Eating, Rumination, and Substance use and abuse. These strategies *do not work*. None leads to an effective shutting down of the amygdala and none results in the absence of fear. In fact, they almost always make fear—and most situations—much worse.

> *The absence of fear is not courage . . . the absence of fear*
> *is some kind of brain damage.*
> —M. Scott Peck

> *If we take the generally accepted definition of bravery as*
> *a quality which knows no fear, I have never seen a brave*
> *man. All men are frightened. The more intelligent they*
> *are, the more they are frightened.*
> —General George S. Patton

Do not be afraid of sudden fear.

—Proverbs 3:25

As we've mentioned before, fear is a gift, rather than something to be avoided. Every animal in nature has a prescribed, built-in, healthy response to fear that is most advantageous for survival and success. So the next logical question becomes: "If the human brain has such a law—*just what is it that we humans are supposed to do when we are afraid?*" I've asked this question to audiences all over the world from Kazakhstan to Guam and no one has ever come up with the correct answer. Before journeying forward, let's pause a moment for you to take your best guess. Then, in the next chapter, we will discover that the human brain does, indeed, have its own law for what it wants us to do when we're afraid—and if we obey this law, we will maximize our chances for good physical health and sustained career and relationship success. What we do when we are afraid, in any life sphere, is *the fork in the road to success.*

CHAPTER 3

The Healthy Response

The Fork in the Road to Success

So just what is this law, this optimal human response to fear? The best evidence, surprisingly, comes from our observations of chimpanzees both in laboratory studies and in the wild. Why these particular primates? Because they share over 90 percent of human DNA and their emotional brains—their midbrains—are most similar to ours. A baby chimp, when frightened, does not run or burrow or fly or attack. Instead, no matter what the threat might be, it reaches to its mother, leaps onto her back or into her arms, and stays there until the amygdala quiets. Adult chimps are similar in their response. In observations in the wild it's been noted that, when facing a threat, chimpanzees consistently make eye contact with one another as a first response before attacking or leaping to safety. To test this, a group of Dutch anthropologists created a mechanical papier-mâché leopard and positioned it to leap in front of a group of chimps, scaring them on their way to a watering hole. How do you think the chimps responded? They all reached for one another, making a connection first, before the two dominate chimps ventured forth to do battle with the paper leopard.

The more I observed these monkeys, the more I became interested in this unique response to fear. I wondered, why was this the primate's instinctive response? In search of an answer, I reviewed Dr. Harry Harlow's controversial early studies with rhesus macaque monkeys. Although distressing to observe, the research was extremely revealing. In these studies, baby monkeys were raised for six months by terry-cloth "mothers" or mothers made out of wire (not very comforting!). While watching the videos, we humans are painfully aware that the mothers are not real. However, they were the only maternal comfort the baby rhesus monkeys had ever known. Each infant became attached to its particular mother, recognizing its face and preferring it above all others. At six months of age, the baby monkeys were suddenly taken from their terry-cloth mothers and placed alone in a room where nothing was moving and there was no sound. The room held only inanimate objects, nothing larger than the monkey, and nothing overtly threatening. The isolation and the unfamiliarity of the room, however, was enough to trigger the small creatures' amygdalas and the terrified animals would crouch into balls, shaking, paralyzed with fear. The researchers found that their amygdalas would never quiet, no matter how long they were alone in the room. Left there, these small animals would have eventually died of fright. Once the familiar mother was reintroduced to the room, however, the young monkeys would leap onto the terry cloth, seeking the comfort necessary to allay their fears. Once reassured of connection, they would then become playful in the room, venturing out once again to explore objects and intermittently retreating to the comfort of their mothers. The monkeys who were provided wire "mothers" or no mother at all—those who never experienced comfort when they reached out—never became accustomed to the room.*

After observing several more films depicting this natural response to fear demonstrated by these primates, the optimal *human* response to fear became abundantly clear. For those of you who are parents, or who were once children (hopefully at least one of these applies to you), I suspect that you may recognize this same adaptive response in our own untrained young as well. Consider this common scenario: when awakened by a nightmare or the frightening sound of thunder, what do young children instinctively do? The answer is universal. In response to such terror, without a moment's hesitation or training, small children will run straight to their parents' bed. The parents typically embrace the child and say in a soothing voice: "It's only a nightmare" or "It's only thunder" in an attempt to calm their fear—as if those words mean anything to a small trembling child! And what does the child do next? He or she falls peacefully back to sleep in the safety of mother or father's arms. Did the doctor teach the infant to do this before leaving the hospital? Of course not! The child knows to do this because it is the natural, optimal human response to fear. *We are meant to reach to another for support. We are suggesting that the Law of Success, the fork in the road to success to is be aware of and accepting of fear and be willing when afraid, to reach to another for support.*

As you consider that thought, let's return to the longitudinal studies mentioned earlier in the Introduction. In each of the investigations—the Kauai, Terman, and Harvard Grant Studies, as well as the Study of Adult Development—it was discovered that a person's ability to reach for support, along with the presence of supportive others in their lives, were critical underlying factors in an individual's long-term success. Take, for example, the high-risk children in the Kauai Longitudinal Study who ended up thriving at ages 18 and 30 despite significant early life challenges. These children, it was noted, had the opportunity to establish a close bond with at least one caretaker from whom they received positive attention during the first years of life. In many cases (like the monkeys raised with terry-cloth mothers), this bond was not with the child's biological parent, but instead a relative, neighbor, baby sitter, or another caring adult who had stepped in to fulfill the nurturing role. The children also tended to be well-liked by their classmates, had at least one close friend, and they seemed to find a great deal of emotional support outside the immediate family. Many of the thriving youth also mentioned a favorite teacher who became a role model, friend, and confidant who was particularly supportive at times when the child's family was beset by discord or threatened with dissolution. As Dr. Werner summarized, "The resilient children had at least one person in their lives who accepted them unconditionally, regardless of temperamental idiosyncrasies or physical or mental handicaps."[1]

Now to some of you, it may appear that *reaching for support* contradicts the basic principles of competition, which many of us believe underlie success and allow some people to thrive to a greater extent than others in today's world. You might be concerned that by purposefully reaching for support, you could interfere with your ability to succeed. There is no denying that individual competition does, in fact, play an essential role in generating some successes in life. For example, we often see competition exert itself meaningfully when we are in the "climbing the ladder" phases of life. You may believe that you got into college because you were smarter than the person sitting next to you in high school, or you may think that you received your advanced degree, or landed a coveted job because you worked harder than other college students or fellow employees. Perhaps you believe that you attracted your mate because you were more powerful, kinder and more compassionate, more physically fit, more intelligent, or better parent material than others around you; or, you may believe that because you've eaten right, exercised regularly, and avoided cigarettes, you've been immune to some of the illnesses others have encountered. On the other hand, maybe you think that others have succeeded more than you did because they demonstrated these sorts of strengths in daily competition.

All of these considerations certainly have some bearing on the truth, and individual competition is definitely important in some stages of and activities in life. However, what many of us don't recognize is that competition doesn't necessarily lead to *sustained* success in any area of life. Once these initial successes are achieved, the time comes when we must collaborate, inspire others to collaborate, ask for help, and allow others to help us in order to grow beyond initial stages to the highest levels of success. Growing up and living in an enriched, caring environment gives a person the freedom and opportunity to practice asking for help and the opportunity to learn to compete or collaborate selectively, whichever might be called for in a given situation. These skills are essential in our adult lives, where collaboration is most often the key to success.

Herbert Spencer first coined the phrase "survival of the fittest"[2] after reading about the concept of natural selection in Charles Darwin's *On the Origin of the Species*. This phrase has often been misunderstood to mean each animal competing with every other animal of the same species for food, territory, and mating privileges. This was not at all what Darwin had in mind. What Darwin wrote was: "In the long history of humankind (and animal kind too) those who learned to collaborate and improvise most effectively have prevailed." He, like many successful individuals past and present, recognized that *reaching for support* is essential in achieving and sustaining long term success.

> *You can't do it all yourself. Don't be **afraid** to rely on others to help you accomplish your goals.*
> —Oprah Winfrey

Consider the following thoughts from other remarkable people who have shared similar insights. Sir Isaac Newton stated it well when he said, "If I have seen further, it is by standing on the shoulder of giants."[3] This was not false modestly, but rather an awareness that his many strengths and successes were due to the support of others. This perspective is the rule, not the exception, for successful individuals. Successful people recognize their need for support and consistently see reaching out to others as a strength rather than a weakness. At the peak of his business success, Henry Ford stated: "I invented nothing new. I simply assembled the discoveries of other men behind whom were centuries of work. Had I worked fifty or ten or even five years before, I would have failed. So it is with every new thing. Progress happens when all the factors that make for it are ready, and then it is inevitable. To teach that a comparatively few men are responsible for the greatest forward steps of mankind is the worst sort of nonsense."[4]

So by now I hope that you are fully convinced that the most critical skill in achieving and sustaining success in all key areas of life is *a willingness, when afraid, to reach for support.* And this relies on our *awareness and acceptance of fear.* In the chapters that follow, we will carefully examine the tremendous impact that "reaching for support" has on our physical health, work success, creativity, and relationships. As mentioned earlier, the bigger and more important the goal, the more fear will be present. And, once you have achieved success, moments will come when you will fear losing it or you will be afraid that you might not deserve it. Reaching for and receiving support when you are facing these fears is essential to getting the reassurance necessary to develop new skills and propel you to the next level of success.

Of all the things I have done, the most vital is coordinating the talents of those who work for us and pointing them towards a certain goal.
—Walt Disney

We don't accomplish anything in this world alone . . . and whatever happens is the result of the whole tapestry of one's life and all the weavings of individual threads from one to another that creates something.
—Sandra Day O'Connor, Supreme Court Justice

It may not be an accident that the word "wealth" starts with "we." For, although the conscious mind typically defines wealth in terms of income, property, and title, the emotional brain is only interested in one thing: "In times of need, who will be there for me?" Because of this, whether business partners, lovers, or life-long friends, the most important thing you want to know about a person before you trust them is *what will they do when they are afraid?*

Whatever the relationship might be, when you hit a bumpy patch and one or both of you get scared, you want to know whether you will reach to each other for help or start arguing, blaming, or disappearing. Take romance, for example. Romance requires a willingness to share your fears with another. Relationships usually begin in fun, but at some point most become scary. This typically happens for one of two reasons. The first is that the person we have invested so much in is not as consistent as we would like them to be. Perhaps they promise they will call while out of town, then insist that they fell asleep before they could get to the phone. Or maybe they have come home too many nights in a row grumpy and tired, and we begin to wonder whether it's really us, rather than work, making them unhappy. The second reason we become fearful in relationships is that things *are* going well—the relationship is wonderful! However, because it's so wonderful, we are afraid that the person might change his or her mind and go away or find someone they like more. Our challenge, in either one of these scary moments, is to go to the very person we are afraid of losing and say, "I was so afraid today, thinking what my life would be like if you went away." And the hope is that, because you have chosen so wisely on the basis of their relationship to fear, they will hold you and say in a loving voice, "I know, I feel that way sometimes too."

This principle applies to any relationship—romantic, family, friends, work, or community. *The most important thing that you need to know about people before you trust them is what they will do when they are afraid.* Will they be there when you reach for support? In a culture such as ours where we've forgotten that we are afraid to cross the street, what are the chances that we will audition our mate, business partner, or friend on the basis of their relationship to fear?

> *Coming together is a beginning, staying together is*
> *progress, and working together is success.*
> —Henry Ford

This section is entitled *The Fork in the Road to Success* to remind us that, although individual competition is at times essential, there is an alternate and more critical skill we must develop if we are to achieve and sustain the success we seek in all key areas of life. As mentioned before, we often must compete against others for opportunities that become harder to achieve as we move through our school years and into adult life. However, at a certain point in our careers, the skills of collaboration, asking for help, and playing well with others become essential. Seeking friends or a lover often requires a degree of assertiveness as well. On the other hand, maintaining intimacy with any person across time requires a willingness to be vulnerable, to share one's emotions, to seek comfort and advice, and a willingness to respond in turn when others reach for support. Having the skills to compete and collaborate, and being adept at switching tactics depending on what the situation calls for, puts us solidly on the path to success.

Highly successful individuals view reaching for and receiving support as a strength. Consider Jeff Bezos, founder of Amazon.com. He regularly reaches out for support within his company in order to help it grow. When asked how Amazon manages to come up with so many brilliant concepts and products, he said that he often writes a two or three page memo and sends it to the executive team for their input. "What I find is, by the time that process is done, I'm never really sure if I've invented something or not, because it starts here and ends up there. That's what you want if you have a bunch of smart people. Somebody says, 'Well, that will never work because you forgot x, y, and z.' And then you step back and realize that's true and then it morphs and builds."[5]

Howard Schultz, the CEO of Starbucks, provides yet another example of a successful person who readily recognizes the support he has received from others. In an article in *Businessweek* magazine, he examines the journey that led to his very successful return to Starbucks, identifying the supporters who helped him along the way. Schultz gives credit to Michael Dell, CEO of Dell computers, for encouraging his return and he credits Jim Senegal of Costco for suggesting strategies to help with Starbucks' resuscitation.[6]

Are you wondering whether or not there are gender differences when it comes to reaching for support? It may appear to some of us that significant dissimilarities exist between the sexes in this area. Some brilliant modern researchers, including Shelley Taylor, PhD, author of *The Tending Instinct*[7] have explored this issue at great length. In her research, Dr. Taylor labeled the skills of providing and reaching for support "tending and befriending." In this, she refers to the protection of those in need (tending) and the seeking out of a social group for mutual defense (befriending). Dr. Taylor does suggest that women may be more likely than men to reach for support.[8] She explains that this greater frequency of occurrence in females may be due to genetics, hormones, and evolution. While males went off to hunt, women gathered food and worked together to raise children and share the tasks of the tribe. In other words, because of the historical roles they've played, they have perhaps had greater opportunity to practice and reap the rewards of reaching for support.

Although the inclination to "tend and befriend" may be more prevalent in women, research supports that it is the tendency of all humans to affiliate, to establish groups, and come together in threatening times, regardless of gender. Reaching for support is the healthy response to fear for both sexes—it is often just expressed differently. Further on in Taylor's book, she provides examples of men's collaborative nature: "Rather than hoarding their kills for their own families, successful hunters commonly shared their meat with the entire group." Taylor's basic thesis is the same as the one explored in this book you are reading: Humans are naked apes, hairless animals who can't outrun anyone, can't defend well against predators, and can't even stay warm without help. Our success as a species has come entirely from our gregarious nature. We live and work together, having found safety in numbers across the many thousands of years of our evolution.

A more dramatic example of the male ability to "tend and befriend" can be found in the innovative research of Dr. Muzafer Sherif, founder of modern social psychology.[9] Dr. Sherif brought groups of boys together in a summer camp setting in order to study the social norms of male group formation, conflict, and conflict resolution. Upon arrival, the boys were placed in two separate cabins. Researcher-counselors noted early on the boys' male tendency to form groups that competed, sometimes harshly, with the boys in the other cabin. To further increase their separation and rivalry, he encouraged each cabin to give themselves names, and he went even further by devising athletic contests and treasure hunts to purposefully intensify the competition. Sherif was amazingly successful in generating conflict and competiveness. As time went on, the boys became increasingly aggressive, raiding each other's cabins, stealing possessions, and exchanging harsh words. Seeing the boys at this stage one might wonder, "Is this simply a result of male biological tendencies being unleased in a *Lord of the Flies* manner?"

Sherif then worked to reverse the process. He began hosting movie nights and other social events, but these initially led to even more conflict, such as food fights and physical attacks. To determine whether this response was reflective of the male's natural response to living in groups, or perhaps just one of many options, Sherif set out to explore this question in a very creative manner. To begin with, the boys were all told that the truck that went to town to get food for the camp was stuck. In order to be fed, the boys were required to work together to help the truck out of its predicament. Next, Sherif arranged to have the camp's water supply interrupted due to a problem with the pipes. Boys from both cabins had to work together to fix this crisis as well. In a third scenario, the boys were looking forward to an upcoming movie night when camp counselors informed them that the budget wouldn't allow for it, so the event would be cancelled. To solve this problem, boys from both cabins pooled their funds to rescue the rental.

You can see where this is heading. Through these shared challenges, the boys learned the value of helping one another out and working together. Across time, the conflict between the two cabins disappeared and boys from different cabins began eating together at meals. Toward the end of the experience, when the boys were asked to list their best friends, their lists frequently contained names from both cabins. On the final bus ride home, during a meal stop, Sherif observed that some of the boys who still had a few dollars left graciously treated boys without funds from the other cabin to milkshakes. Giving and receiving support, then, became the natural response when the "tribes" faced mutual challenges, just as it did for our ancestors, who learned as they walked the savannah that mutual cooperation and support was essential for survival. This remains true for all of us today. Reaching out, in any life sphere, is the fork in the road to success.

'Note: It is worth stating that the types of primate studies we are referencing here are now illegal. The research was completed at a time when there was little discussion of animal rights. However, these studies are referenced here, because they did reveal important information and we owe it to ourselves and our primate relatives to learn from all that they were subjected to at an earlier time.

CHAPTER 4

Mastering Fear

Fundamentally the world is uncertain. Decisions are about the future and your place in the future when the future is uncertain. So what is the key thing you can do to prepare for that uncertainty? You can have the right people with you.

—Jim Collins

What Do You Reach For?

I hope by now you are convinced that when you are afraid, reaching for support is a good—a very good—idea. Taking action, however, is always more challenging than knowing that something is true. If you are old enough to be reading this book, I imagine that by now you have already discovered some reason to ignore, question, or challenge everything I have said about reaching for support. It's likely that at some point in your life someone has betrayed you and broken your heart. Maybe a friend has said you could trust them and you learned painfully that this was not the case. Or perhaps someone at work has ignored, refused, or even ridiculed you when you have reached out. We have all experienced such rejection, and there's little in life that hurts worse than that. So, if you decide that you're ready to revisit this crucial skill, you'll need a new set of tools in place to set you up for success.

To help you with this, let me start by sharing a story that may at first seem to be completely unrelated. At the end of the Vietnam War, I was living and working in Fresno, California. For those readers too young to remember (and those of you old enough to have forgotten), a time came in the war when South Vietnam was overrun by the North. In response, the United States gathered some of the Southern Vietnamese people who worked for us onto transports and moved them rapidly out of the country. These refugees were flown to various cities throughout the United States, including Fresno. Each evening, I watched on TV as these new Americans exited the plane looking exhausted and relieved, and I watched again as they settled into government housing and work, appearing enterprising and grateful.

Not long after their arrival, however, I noticed some bizarre scenes playing out in our local grocery stores. On more than one occasion as I pushed my cart through the bakery section, I witnessed Vietnamese families—fathers and mothers, usually with one or two children in tow—staring silently at the bread display, immovable and weeping. This strange scene, inexplicable to me at the time, made sense to me much later as I learned more about human beings' natural response to isolation and fear. All of these people were strong, brave individuals who had lived through night-mares that most of us, fortunately, could never imagine. They had been catapulted into this foreign land where, from the moment they exited the airplane, everything in life—the language, the cur-rency, the customs, and the bread—was unfamiliar and strange, utterly different from what they'd previously experienced. Rice, not bread, had been their family's main staple. And here they were, trapped in a grocery store aisle, besieged with fear as they stood staring at hundreds of choices in bread products with absolutely no idea as to what they should select to sustain their hungry families.

When most Americans go into the bakery section, on the other hand, their brains instantly have access to a lifetime of memo-ries related to bread. We are indeed "gourmets" when it comes to selecting what we might need for any occasion: wheat, rye, or sour-dough; bagels, croissants, or baguettes; hoagie rolls or hamburger buns, with and without seeds. These newly arrived refugees, how-ever, had no stored memories of bread to draw upon in order to solve the problem of feeding their families. For some of them, this was the last straw added to an overwhelming stack of feelings they had experienced as they sought to live in this strange new world they had entered so quickly. Of course, a year later, most of them were successful consumers of bread just like you and I!

So what is the point of this story? What does the selection of bread have to do with developing our awareness of fear and our ability and willingness to reach for support? Quite a bit, actually.

If you were a person who grew up with a great deal of nurturing from loving parents, grandparents, neighbors, teachers, scout or religious leaders, etc., then when those times in life come when you are afraid and in need of support, you likely have some idea of what kind of support you might need and from whom you are most likely to get it. If, however, like the Vietnamese families with no memories of bread, you were raised with very little healthy support at home or in the community, then even if you are wise and courageous enough to realize that you need help, you may not know exactly what kind you need or who might be best able to provide it. In these circumstances, your chances of getting effective support (the amount and kind you really need) are simply that—a chance.

Even those who have experienced high-quality support in the past may find that reaching for support is challenging in new situations. This may be especially true when you are developing new relationships in unfamiliar environments, where past supporters are not available, or when you have no related memories to help you identify what kind of support you might need in that moment. This may occur, for example, when you are feeling isolated in a new job, new locale, or in a new romance or family situation. In these cases, asking for support may seem unfamiliar and strange. However, whether you have a history of many encouraging, helpful individuals in your past, or a paucity of warm, supportive people preceding this moment, we now know that *all* human beings best master fear and achieve greatest success when we reach to others for support. Therefore, it is essential that all of us be well-equipped.

Instead of leaving this critical skill to chance, it may be best if we have a guide. Before I provide you with that, however, take just a minute to complete the following exercise, which is designed to assess how "gourmet" you might already be when it comes to reaching for support.

Think of one person in your life, past or present, who has supported you well; a person without whom some of your greatest opportunities or qualities may never have been realized. Now, as specifically as possible, describe the type of support they gave. How did this person get through your lack of awareness or knowledge, your fear or reticence, your independence, stubbornness, or pride to move your life in a way you could not have imagined?

How easy was it for you to clearly describe the type(s) of support that worked for you in your moment(s) of need? If more than one person or situation came to mind, I suspect that you are becoming increasingly aware that, not only do different situations call for varied types of support, but that certain people in your life tend to be the right ones to provide those specific types of support. Recognizing these two things is essential in knowing who you should turn to when you are facing any fear and you are in need of support.

A Gourmet Guide to Support

The following menu is a "gourmet guide" that describes the many different types of support we may need at varying times in life.

You can use this guide to become more aware of the types of support you might want to ask others for in various life situations, or you can use it in your role as a parent, teacher, coworker, supervisor, mate, or friend when you try out different types of support when the person you want to help, like one of those distraught families in the bread aisle, is unaware of what to ask for.

To help you recall the many possible types of support, let's use the mnemonic INSPIRE. In the human body, the word *inspire* means "to take in." When you think about it, this is exactly what we are doing when we ask for and receive support. We are receiving—taking in—the gifts bestowed by another. Emotionally, *inspire* means to "motivate and encourage." This, too, is what we do when we provide support to others, and it is typically how we feel when others provide support to us. For these reasons, INSPIRE is ideal for helping us to recall the various types of support.

Types of Support
Instruction
Nurturing
Spirituality
Praise
Inquisitiveness
Rejection
Example

Instruction: This is perhaps the most obvious type of support. Most of us can recall some point or another in our lives where others have provided us this kind of support. Instruction is "served up" in three different ways: *information, resources,* and *skills. Information* is exactly what it sounds like. It is the act of communicating stored knowledge to others. *Resources* refers to making supplies available for use when needed. *Skills* are talents or abilities, typically acquired through experience or training, that can be shared with others. For example, if you want to learn more about computers, you might become informed in any one of the three ways. You could attend a lecture on the various types of computers available, their uses, how they are assembled, or how a new software program works (*instruction*). Alternately, you might be placed in front of a new computer or a program where you can explore for yourself how to use them (*resources*). In yet another scenario, you might have an instructor or friend, a computer "mentor" of some kind, sitting beside you and walking you through the learning process (*skills*). Each of these forms of instruction can provide very beneficial support for you or others at different times in life.

Nurturing: We define nurturing as *the ability to listen empathically, compassionately, without the need to give advice or suggestions.* Nurturing also means to provide sustenance or care. As described in Chapter 3, this type of support is essential for the developing monkey—and for the developing and full grown human being as well. If you have ever experienced a life crisis such as the loss of a job, a serious illness, a divorce, or the death of a loved one, you may recall that many of your friends were wonderful in the various ways they nurtured and supported you. But you may also remember one or two friends who appeared insensitive and/or said some very foolish things. It was probably not that they were truly callous individuals or that they didn't care about you or your situation. Instead, it is likely that your situation caused fear and they didn't have the experience or skills to respond in a more thoughtful way. To be comfortable with and helpful to someone from whom life has ripped away something precious, you must go inside yourself and remember (or imagine, if you have not had a similar experience) how painful those circumstances would be for you. Some people are afraid or unable to go to that painful place, so in emotional situations they say unexpected or thoughtless things in an attempt to fix something that is beyond the human capacity to repair.

The following quote was written by Henri Nouwen for cancer patients, but I believe it applies to any serious life challenge and every friendship: "The friend who can be silent with us in a moment of despair or confusion, who can stay with us in an hour of grief and bereavement, who can tolerate not knowing, not curing, not healing, and face with us the reality of our powerlessness, that is a friend who cares."[1]

Whether in the form of a listening ear, a hand on the shoulder, a meaningful e-mail, letter, or gift, an extra moment or many moments across time, nurturing is yet another essential form of support that underlies success in all key areas of life.

Spirituality: For some of us, help of any kind comes always from one primary source—a universal, divine spirit. Whether provided by a good friend, a caring doctor, a loving pet, or circumstance, all forms of support are considered gifts from God. For individuals with these beliefs, prayer is often an instinctive response to fear and a means of reaching for the ultimate form of support. Ministers, priests, rabbis, or other spiritual leaders, as well as fellow congregation members, are often considered manifestations of a holy presence. These people and the places they congregate are additional sources where spiritual people can reach for and receive needed support.

A powerful description of spirituality as a vital form of support comes from Joan Borysenko in her book *Guilt is the Teacher, Love is the Lesson*: "When we are absolutely miserable, prayer is no longer a dry rote repetition. It becomes a living and vibrant cry for help. It becomes authentic. In pain, we forget the 'thees' and the 'thous' that keep us separated from God, and reach a new state of intimacy that comes from talking to God in our own way, saying what's in our heart."[2]

In a more secular example, actor Denzel Washington shares his sense of spiritual support in the following way: "Yes, I've worked hard. I made some sacrifices until I finally made it. Yes, you could say I had some luck. But I also had tremendous help along the way. That was a huge blessing from God. Behind every great success, there's someone. And often more than one person. A parent, teacher, coach, role model . . . it starts somewhere."[3]

For those individuals who consider themselves religious or spiritual, a divine spirit is the first, most essential place to reach for support and the most likely to be able to provide exactly what's needed in any situation. For these individuals, all human or material support are gifts from God and reaching beyond the human capacity to provide support may be what is needed in many of life's most challenging situations.

Praise: This type of support is provided by people who, on those days when we feel small and inadequate, insist on telling us how wonderful we are while we squirm and protest the whole time. These are the mentors who make us feel special and remind us of our goodness, quite often when we are not getting the results in the world that we are seeking. The reach for this type of support can be seen in children who call unabashedly, "Mommy, mommy, look at me!" as they conquer playground equipment or bring home from school a work of art. Adults, too, require praise from those we respect and those who love us. It is yet another essential form of support underlying success.

Praise can be empowering, a way to help people sustain effort and enthusiasm, both in times of success and times of challenge. However, the specific type of praise given is critical to the outcome. In children, for example, research has demonstrated that some types of praise are empowering, while others can be crippling. Dr. Carol Dweck, a psychology professor at Stanford and author of *Mindset: The New Psychology of Success*, has illuminated the power and peril of praise in her insightful research.[4] What she discovered was that praising children for effort (for example, "You worked really hard at this, I am proud of you for your effort.") sets them up for a lifetime of enthusiastic learning and encourages them in developing the underlying skills necessary for seeking and overcoming challenges. Praising them for their gifts or qualities (for example, "You are so talented, so smart," etc.), on the other hand, predisposes many toward a life of risk-avoidance and self-doubt.[5] Experimentation and trial-and-error learning threatens these children's identities as gifted, talented, brilliant individuals.

One of Dr. Dweck's most compelling studies clearly illustrates the power of both healthy and unhealthy praise. The subjects were 400 New York 5th graders, all who were given a simple puzzle to complete where their success was virtually guaranteed. After completing this task, half of the test group were complimented for their effort (for example, "You must have worked very hard."), whereas the other 200 were praised for their personality (for example, "You must be smart at this."). That was it—one compliment, from one stranger, for one task. Seemingly inconsequential. However, when they looked at the impact of these two types of support, they realized that the outcome was quite profound. During the next stage of the study, all of the students were offered a choice: either another easy puzzle like the first one or a more challenging puzzle. More than 50 percent of the children who were praised for their intelligence (their personalities) chose the easy one. On the other hand, more than 90 percent of the children who had been praised for working hard chose the more difficult puzzle. The researchers hypothesized the children choosing the easier task likely did so to increase the chance of proving to themselves and the examiner once again how smart they were. The comment regarding effort gave the other children the support they needed to risk tackling harder tasks, because they knew that they would be supported more for their attempts than for the outcome.

In the final stage of the research, the impact of the type of praise became even more noticeable. All of the students were given a very hard puzzle—one where failure was practically certain and they would know it from the start. This was followed by a very easy task, quite similar to the first one. So what was the outcome? The "praised-for-intelligence" group scores declined by 20 percent, whereas the "praised-for-effort" group scores increased by 30 percent. Astoundingly, this single compliment from a stranger sharing the message "you are smart" vs. "you work hard" resulted in shaking a child's identity to the core in the face of any potential setback.

Following this research, Dweck identified two different mind-sets that evolve as a result of adult messages. Children praised for effort typically develop a "growth mindset." They assume that success is a result of hard work and persistence and that difficulties are to be expected. These children embrace their mistakes and assume that challenges are part of the learning process. Because of this, they are more comfortable identifying deficiencies and taking steps to address them. Dr. Dweck encourages parents in this approach, remarking in *Mindset: The New Psychology of Success*: "If parents want to give their children a gift, the best thing they can do is teach their children to love challenges, be intrigued by mistakes, enjoy effort, and keep on learning. That way, their children don't have to be slaves of praise. They will have a life-long opportunity to build and repair their own confidence."

The second type of mindset Dweck identified was a "fixed mindset." These children were told, often repeatedly, that they were gifted, talented, and bright. Children presented with this message are apt to see their talents as fixed qualities and they expect themselves to succeed in any activity they participate in. They do not tend to seek out or tolerate criticism, because this challenges their identities as innately gifted. They do not expect difficulties and, when they occur, these children are inclined to blame situations or others (for example, the poor test or the lousy teacher) instead of taking responsibility, embracing their mistakes, and taking action to address them. They often act superior to keep from feeling inferior. You may, in fact, know a person like this—someone who never is, and never can be, wrong.

The takeaway message here is that praise can be a powerful form of support in the right circumstances, especially when it sends the message "keep trying!" This is important for not only children, but adults as well. Based on her work with staff at Silicon Valley companies, Dr. Dweck suggests that we might best provide support to other adults by praising them for actions such as taking initiative, seeing a difficult task through, struggling and learning something new, being undaunted by a setback, and being open and acting on criticism.

Studies on successful marriages also reveal the effect that attention and praise have with adults. One of the foremost experts in the world in marriage research is John Gottman, PhD, author of *Why Marriages Succeed and Fail*.[6] What makes his work remarkable is that he can interview engaged couples for just 15 minutes or less and predict, with 90 percent success, the likelihood that they will be happily married vs. miserable or divorced four years later. He boils it down to two key predictors. The first is how couples deal with conflict. This is not surprising, because conflicting perspectives will certainly arise from time to time between two individuals living in close quarters. The second predictor is whether their positive attention outweighs their negative interactions on a daily basis by a factor of five positive to one negative on the days the relationship isn't going well, and 20 to one on the days the relationship is thriving. When he speaks of "positive attention," do you think he is referring to 20 candlelight dinners or 20 walks on the beach holding hands? Hardly. He is referring to small moments. For example, does your voice light up when you mate calls you during the day or does your tone of voice imply that your beloved is interrupting more important tasks? Do you put down the remote control, newspaper, or cell phone and greet your partner enthusiastically when s/he walks through the door? Do you compliment his or her parenting skills or the way s/he treats your parents? Surprisingly, Dr. Gottman found that these small acts of acknowledgement were more important than anything else the couple could do!

> *Make individuals feel important and part of something larger than themselves.*
> —General Colin Powell

Consider and respond to the following questions:

1. Do you have someone in your life who is genuine and generous with their praise? If so, when do they compliment you? Do you enjoy the compliment or do you fight it and try to convince the person they are wrong?
2. Are there particular compliments that you prefer from each important person in your life?
3. Imagine a friend, lover, or boss (choose only one to start) and once or twice each day ask yourself, "If I could have the exact compliment I would like to have from that person at this moment, what would it be?"

Inquisitiveness: Asking good questions is an essential type of support in many situations. You probably already have some good instincts when it comes to recognizing a good question. For example, when you go to a friend or professional for help, do they ask questions that invite you to look inside yourself to find answers and resources you did not know you had? If so, that individual recognizes the power of inquisitiveness when people are afraid and in need of support.

It is the rare person who has the skill to ask questions that do not imply an opinion or judgment. Once others sense that you have already formed an opinion, they're likely to become defensive rather than reflective. For example, if I were to ask, "Why are you wearing that outfit today?" or "Why didn't you complete that project Friday?" my intent may be sincere. I may actually be curious as to why you chose that specific ensemble or interested in what might have prevented you from finalizing your exciting work on time. However, "why" questions like these often cause people to justify their behavior rather than examine a situation more thoroughly. If inquisitiveness is to be used meaningfully in response to another's reach for support, it is essential that the questions be genuinely that—*inquisitive.*

> *The most important and difficult job is never to find the right answers, it is to find the right question.*
> —Peter Drucker

The following exercise will help you to become more aware of how skillful you are at giving others this kind of support.

Seek out someone whose political opinion is very different than your own and introduce a topic that you have strong feelings about. Next, ask your partner 10 open-ended, genuine questions that demonstrate curiosity and do not give the impression you have any specific feelings on the subject. You will know that you are succeeding when the other person starts becoming more animated and enthusiastic about sharing their opinion with you.

I have shared this exercise with people from many walks of life and from many different professions, including doctors, lawyers, engineers, teachers, students, and others. Every one of them has found that asking good questions can be exceedingly difficult. For those of us who want to become experts (or even those who want to be just pretty darn good) at providing this type of support, it will take a lot of practice. As a matter of fact, I try to practice at least once each week to maintain my awareness and improve my proficiency with this skill.

For example, recently I had the opportunity to practice while traveling from Tucson to Los Angeles, typically about a one hour flight. I was sitting next to a woman and, as the flight began, we struck up a conversation. I asked her what she planned to do while she was in L.A. She replied that she wasn't staying in California, but was changing planes and from there was on her way to Africa. Interested, I asked: "What are you planning to do when you arrive there?" She said that it was her 87th birthday and she was going on a Safari. "A photography safari?" I queried. "No, a hunting safari," she said. I was quite surprised! She certainly didn't fit my stereotype of a big game hunter. Nor, I admitted to myself, was killing a wild animal from 500 yards away my personal idea of a good time. I could have spent the rest of the trip trying to convince her of my point of view and, in the process, likely take some of the joy out of her birthday journey. However, I didn't see much point in that. Instead, I decided to practice asking good questions. Given my strong feelings on the subject, I wondered whether I would be able to ask genuine questions, ones that would allow me to understand what made this activity so important to her, without revealing my perspective. As my new friend became more animated sharing her story with me, I was certain that my practice had been successful.

In his bestselling book *Good to Great*, Jim Collins refers to the importance of asking genuine questions in the work setting as well: "The good-to-great leaders made particularly good use of informal meetings, where they'd meet with groups of managers and employees with no script, agenda, or set of action items to discuss. Instead they would start with questions like: 'So what's on your mind?' or 'Can you tell me more about that?' These non-agenda meetings became a forum for current realities to bubble to the surface."[7] The importance of asking good questions has been mentioned in the world of sports as well. John Wooden, UCLA Basketball Coach, remarked: "Most leaders don't listen and yet it is one of the greatest methods we have of learning. You need to listen to those under your supervision and to those who are above you. We'd all be a lot wiser if we listened more—not just hearing the words, but listening and not thinking about what we're going to say."[8] The important thing to recognize is that, no matter what the life setting, asking and answering good questions is essential in achieving success and in providing support to help others succeed.

Following is a list of questions and phrases you may want to "try on" as you learn to become more genuinely inquisitive. These are supportive in many situations, and may be especially helpful when you are upset or when perspectives differ:

- Can you help me understand? What are your thoughts about _____?
- I'd like to know more about this.
- Have you always felt this way? How did you come to look at the issue this way?
- That's really interesting. Can you tell me more about _____?
- How would you respond to people who say _____?
- Is it okay if I ask you about _____?
- Please tell me how I can learn more.

If you are on the receiving end of this type of support, have you chosen someone to help you who has this skill?

Rejection: Do you have someone in your life who is willing to let you know when they think you're off course, and who is able to tell you in such a way that you can really hear? This type of support is vital to our success. In order to grow, and in order to be sure our points of view are correct, we need to seek out and listen to those who don't agree with us. One of the most successful businessmen in the world, John Mackey, CEO of Whole Foods, puts it this way: "I actually think you should engage your critics and see them, too, as stakeholders who are helping you grow."[9] The same idea is shared by James Lapine, film director with 11 Tony nominations: "It's easier with a partner. You're not naked, alone. And you have someone to ask, 'Am I wrong?' "[10]

Inviting in alternate perspectives and offering differing viewpoints is not an easy task. It can be very difficult to seek out or provide this kind of support for others. A wonderful example of someone who has inspired me greatly in his response to critical feedback is Dr. Martin Seligman. One of Dr. Seligman's original claims to fame was his research underlying the principles of "learned helplessness." His studies demonstrated that when subjects, both human and animal, were repeatedly exposed to a frustrating experience from which there was no escape, two out of three will simply give up. They become helpless within the test situation, so that even when they are provided a possible way out, they remain passive and inactive. This appeared to be a potentially powerful model for how depression works, so Dr. Seligman was invited to share his findings with the faculty at Oxford University—a tremendous honor indeed. The audience was very impressed with his research, with the exception of one psychologist, Dr. John Teasdale. In front of this distinguished and prestigious audience, Teasdale shared his criticism: "How can Seligman explain that one out of three humans, dogs, etc., never gave up and, as soon as a new opportunity arose, they leapt into action? You really shouldn't be carried away by this enchanting story. The theory is wholly inadequate. Seligman has glossed over the fact that one-third of his animal and human subjects never became helpless. Why not?"

I fear that if this had happened to me, being thoroughly embarrassed in this public and professional arena, I would have become angry and defensive. But here is how Seligman reacted:

> When John Teasdale raised his objections after my speech at Oxford, I felt for a moment as if years of work might have been for nothing. I had no way of knowing at the time that Teasdale's challenge was the thing I wanted most of all—using our findings to help needful and suffering human beings. Leaving the hall with Teasdale after the address, I asked him if he'd be willing to work with me to see if we could construct an adequate theory. He agreed and we began to meet regularly.[11]

The result of Dr. Seligman's ability to accept support in the form of rejection, along with the psychologists' subsequent collaboration, was the highly regarded work *Learned Optimism*, a national bestseller that provides breakthrough strategies on how to live an optimistic life and help raise an optimistic child.

Seligman's response to rejection—to constructive criticism— is the rule, rather than the exception, for successful people in any endeavor or in any walk of life. For example, what profession could be more solitary than that of an artist? If we believe, "This surely this is a place where individuals flourish without the need of support," we would find ourselves in error. It is simply not true. Picasso and Braque, two of the world's great cubist painters, worked side by side, criticizing each other's work and sharing ideas for half a decade. This collaboration and their willingness to embrace ideas other than their own was a critical factor in their ultimate success, and essential for us in all key areas of life as well. In our work, in relationships, when pursuing improvements in our health or growth in our creativity, rejection is a critical component in helping us to grow and succeed.

It is important to remember that most successful people find criticism just as painful as everyone else. However, in order to grow, successful people embrace the gifts of meaningful rejection and they purposefully reach for support by soliciting feedback from others with varied perspectives. And, they reach out once again if they believe that their critic may be right. Rejection is such an important form of support, in fact, that we've divided it into three types: *refusal, reframing,* and *referral.*

Refusal: This type of support is provided by those who are willing to say "no" to you when they believe that what you are doing will not serve you well. For example, one reason we are all successful to some degree is that our parents were willing to support us by saying no to our childhood preferences for bedtime, food choices, homework vs. play, etc. By saying no, they helped us to develop the discipline and values needed to survive and succeed as adults in today's world. In adulthood, we often find that those with some emotional pull in our lives—family members and close friends, or those with some authority, such as employers, coaches, esteemed colleagues—may all serve to provide this type of support when needed. In similar roles, many of us are called upon to provide this type of support to others as well.

When you are providing support to others by refusing them— by saying no or by sharing important feedback—remember that your tone of voice is generally much more important than the specific words you use. If your voice communicates caring and concern, people can more readily hear and receive the message. If your tone is judgmental or unkind, or if you are upset, frustrated, or angry when you share your feedback, your listener isn't as likely to hear what you say; instead, he or she will be more apt to respond to the meaning implied by your voice. Findings of a recent workplace study provide evidence of the impact of tone of voice when delivering a refusal to staff members. In this experiment, managers were asked to give their employees negative feedback, but they were trained to do so in a warm voice. The employees were later asked how they felt about the feedback and, instead of being defensive, they responded positively, to both the criticism and as evidenced by the changes they made in their work. This is not surprising. Tone is especially important when it comes to communicating people's feelings and attitudes and most research suggests that, *when words and tone of voice don't match, people will generally believe the message communicated by tone.*

For most of us (count me in), saying "no" to people by giving or receiving critical feedback is difficult. This is true even when we have the best intentions and our tone is ideal. I've provided a few suggestions here that might be helpful to you when "refusal" is the best form of support you can ask for or provide to others:

- *Be prompt.* When your feedback is in response to a specific incident, the timing of the conversation should be as close to the event as possible. Otherwise, people may respond to your thoughtful response with, "So why didn't you tell me sooner?" Worse, if you delay, they might begin to assume that you're harboring additional criticisms that you have not yet voiced. This can lead to unnecessary feelings of fear and distrust. Prompt refusals and feedback allow others to reflect and respond when the topic is fresh and the feedback most meaningful.

- *Be specific.* Vague feedback can leave a listener frustrated. General comments such as, "You're too young (or old) to do that" or "You need to improve your project" or "Our marriage needs work," may result in listeners ignoring the most important factors in a refusal. Worse, in an attempt to appease you and reduce their own fears, they may start making changes that are not in their best interest or yours. This can have a significantly negative effect on the individual's success, making things worse for them rather than better, and possibly damaging your relationship in the process. When specific concerns and suggestions are shared, the person receiving feedback will be better able to modify his or her actions or ideas, or let you know clearly that he or she can't or won't.

- *Cultivate a history of praise and appreciation.* Tell others often what is good about them, what you appreciate about them, and what they are doing right. If people feel consistently valued and safe, they are more likely to be able to accept criticism.

Being on the receiving end of criticism, of course, can be quite difficult for anyone. Here are some suggestions that may support you in graciously accepting and considering critical feedback from others:

- Thank them! Even if your heart is pounding and your stomach is in a knot, recognize that the other person is giving you valuable information. Even if you are absolutely certain they are wrong, they are letting you know how your actions and ideas are seen from their—and perhaps others'—perspective.
- Accept responsibility. Being defensive never leads to success. Assume that you could do *something* to improve the situation, even when you believe the other party is at fault.
- Ask for suggestions. You have nothing to lose and everything to gain. You are not obligated to act on their recommendations, but you might find them interesting to consider.
- If there is any kernel of truth in their criticism, reach out and ask them to help you improve.

Reframing: This type of rejection occurs when a person doesn't reject another person's behavior, but instead rejects their interpretation of it. Let me share with you two examples. First, let's revisit an example shared earlier. Imagine that a close friend starts to cry in front of you, then apologizes, saying, "Oh, I am so sorry for crying. You must think I am such a weakling!" When reframing, you don't reject the crying, you reject the person's judgment of it. You might respond by saying, "That's not true. It only makes me feel closer to you that you are willing to share your sadness with me." Another good example of reframing comes from my own childhood experience. My father traveled a lot when I was kid. He was stern, so when he was home he was not generally someone I felt safe confiding in. One day, however, while we were driving somewhere together, I suddenly began to cry. It surprised me as much as it did my dad. He asked, "Why are you crying son?" I didn't stop to measure the risk I was taking. I just blurted out, "Dad, I think I'm ugly." I know that if he'd said that I wasn't, it wouldn't have helped at all. Instead, he became inquisitive, asking "What makes you think you're ugly?" I found the courage to confess. "It's 'cause my ears are so big." Again, if he said that this wasn't true, it would have had no positive effect. Wisely, however, he reframed my despair, saying, "Don't worry son, your head will grow." Perfect logic to an 8-year-old boy! My dad, to this day, does not recall the event, but it is one of my most precious memories of childhood and my favorite example of refusal by reframing.

Referral: This is the type of support you give when someone reaches out to you and you know that you are not the best person to help with that problem. A good example of this might be when a colleague comes to you complaining about another employee and you refer them back to that person, suggesting that it might be best if they dealt with one another directly. In a more challenging situation, perhaps a friend seeks you out to talk about significant relationship problems or alcohol struggles. In this case, it is clear in your mind, that you are not the right person to be attempting to help with something this critical, so you internally reject yourself as the source of support and gently guide them toward the help you think is more useful.

Rejection is a challenging, although essential, form of support in many life situations. Whether it's presented as a direct refusal, reframing, or a referral, we all need people in our lives who are willing and able to tell us "no" or say to us, "Look at this again from another angle" in such a way that we can hear.

Example: This type of support comes from a person who, by the way they are in the world, is someone you want to be like. For many people, this is the most important type of support. It is difficult to take advice from someone you don't respect, even if you know that the person is right. However, when suggestions come from those we look up to, especially in the form of example, we are more likely to make decisions and changes that lead to success. Supportive examples may include a parent or grandparent, teacher or coach, physician or perhaps another remarkable person in your daily life. Or, they could be leaders in business, politics, sports, science, or other areas of professional or personal interest, from history or in the news; perhaps figures of considerable heart and courage, such as Mother Teresa or Nelson Mandela.

> *You can preach a better sermon with your life than your lips.*
>
> —Oliver Goldsmith

We all provide an example for someone and we often provide this form of support without even realizing it. As George Lucas put it: "In almost everything you do, you teach, whether you are aware of it or not. Some people aren't aware of what they are teaching. They should be wiser. Everybody teaches all the time."[12]

An example is someone you want to model your life after, or perhaps something you want to be for someone else. You may agree with Albert Einstein when he said: "Setting an example is not the main means of influencing others, it is the only means."[13]

So this is your gourmet guide. INSPIRE is not intended to provide a complete list of all possible types of support. It is a starters manual, providing a menu of options for you to choose from when you are trying to figure out exactly what you might need or what you might want to offer someone else in need of support. There are, of course, many other types of support. For example, one important type is *human touch*. A warm hug, holding another's hand, or simply placing your hands on a person can be a powerful source of support. Before moving on, take just a minute to reflect on any other forms of support that might not be on our list. *Did you notice that, when it comes to seeking support, people can be very resourceful?* A study by Mark Rosenbaum, a psychologist at Northern Illinois University, demonstrated this human ingenuity in seeking and finding support. His research explored the "social sustenance" of 83 faithful customers at a coffee shop named Kippy's in Chicago. Most of the study subjects were 65 years of age or older. Dr. Rosenbaum assessed where these patrons turned for three specific types of support: *social* (someone to do activities with), *emotional* (someone to discuss problems with), and *instrumental* (someone to help with tasks). What he found was that 60 percent of those who were divorced or widowed sought all three types of support from other diners at Kippy's where they ate multiple times a week. To become and remain successful, all of us need all three types of support somewhere in our lives.[14]

The gourmet guide provides a good first step in helping you to become an expert in reaching for support. If you are going to ask for help when you need it, it is useful to know what kind of support you might want. The likelihood of receiving the support you need increases dramatically with your "menu" in hand. Once you have this awareness, your next step is to identify who in your world is able and most likely to offer that kind of support. Of course, neither knowing what kind of help you need, nor wisely choosing someone who has the skills to support you, guarantees that you will consistently receive the support you seek. The person you choose may be having a hard day, may not be available, or may simply not know how or may not want to provide the support. There is always some risk in asking for help, and receiving help is never 100 percent certain. For this reason, many people are afraid and they hesitate to ask or never reach out at all. This is a mistake. To be successful, choose as wisely as you can, *then take the risk and reach.*

Cultural differences may also influence who we choose to turn to for help and who might be most receptive to the help we have to offer. Let me share a dramatic example. In January, 1989, an unspeakable tragedy occurred in the schoolyard of the Cleveland Elementary School in Stockton, California. A lone gunman stole onto the playground with a semiautomatic rifle and murdered five children, all refugees from Southeast Asia whose parents had come to the United States to provide their children with a better life. The school was soon flooded with counselors, and psychotherapy was made available to the many children and teachers who had witnessed this horror. This form of support was welcomed by many families and teachers. However, for the largely Cambodian community, being offered this type of help was bewildering. They certainly recognized the need for support, but instead sought out friends, families, or their monk for the solace they needed. They found the idea of having such intimate conversations with a stranger rather strange itself.[15,16] Individuals, families, and cultures have varying rituals defining who and how it is acceptable to ask for help. Sometimes it is very clear. Other times it is only evident when the support offered is not acceptable or accepted.

The following exercise will help you to become more aware of who you might reach to when you are in need and how adept you currently are at asking for and accepting different types of support.

Consider and respond to the following questions:

1. Do you see yourself as a "life-long learner," always seeking new information and skills?
2. Do you have family members, friends, colleagues, or mentors who will tell you if they think you are making poor choices?
3. When someone shares critical feedback, is your first response to defend yourself or to ask them for more feedback?
4. Do you see asking for help as a sign of strength or weakness?
5. If you are a manager or supervisor, how have you (or how could you) make it safe for your staff to bring their fears, doubts, and mistakes to you?

6. Do you seek information and suggestions from a diverse group of advisors or do you consistently seek out like-minded people?
7. When you ask for advice, do you secretly hope that the other person will simply agree with and praise you, or are you sincerely seeking input?
8. When sharing a problem or mistake with a trusted advisor, do you tell them everything?
9. When you ask for help, do you let the other person know what specific type of help you are looking for?
10. Do you have at least one friend who asks good questions and does not judge you when you are struggling?
11. Whom do you allow to see you and hold you when you cry?

Although our gourmet guide is a helpful tool, more important is our awareness that help is needed and our courage in seeking it out. Abraham Lincoln provides us with a powerful closing example of how reaching for support can lead to great success. In Doris Kearns Goodwin's prize-winning book *Team of Rivals* she describes Lincoln's extraordinary gift of collaboration. She pointed out that every member of the administration was better known, better educated, and more experienced in public life than Lincoln. "Their presence in the cabinet," she said, "might have threatened to eclipse the obscure prairie lawyer." However, when Lincoln was asked why he had assembled a cabinet including so many opponents who had been harsh with him, he responded: "We needed the strongest men of the party in our cabinet. I had no right to deprive the country of their services."[17] All of us need such people in our lives as well.

As mentioned before, no matter how aware you are of the support you need and no matter how wise you are in your choice of who you reach for, there is always some risk that the person may not respond or respond out of character. There is always some risk of being hurt. Do not let this fear stand in the way of your reaching out. This is the path to mastering fear and achieving the success you desire in all key areas of life. As Abraham Lincoln said, "It is better to trust and be disappointed once in awhile, than to distrust and be miserable all of the time."[18]

CHAPTER 5

Staying Healthy

We have inherited our miraculous bodies from our great, great ancestors, the hunter-gatherers. As we mentioned earlier, the amygdala was absolutely essential for our survival early in our history because it alerted our bodies to the many environmental threats of the time, such as charging lions and hostile spears. Although it is not impossible to encounter such challenges these days, civilization has now protected most of us from these frequent, life-threatening emergencies. There are exceptions of course. We have all, at some point or another, found ourselves suddenly jamming on our brakes to prevent running into the car in front of us, or reaching out desperately to catch some precious object that has just slipped through our fingers. Most of the time, however, our threats unravel slowly, lasting hours, days, weeks, or months at a time rather than the seconds or minutes it would take for a lion to catch and consume us. Because of this, our fight or flight response (which we now know is *fear*) becomes constant and our alarm systems stay on for long periods of time, causing a high risk of physical damage to the very areas of the body designed to escape danger. This persistent state of activation is what we call a *stress disorder.*

When the amygdala is activated for long periods of time, our immune responses are lowered and our bodies become more vulnerable to intruders such as germs and viruses, as well as other more insidious, less obvious illnesses. It is thought that the immune system is impaired during times of stress (persistent fear) because the ancient amygdala believes we are fighting off dangers such as poisonous snakes. It sends all of our protective energy to the bodily functions necessary to respond to those sorts of attacks, and is much less interested in providing energy to the systems that fight illness and disease. To achieve and sustain physical health, then, we must shut the amygdala down and prevent it from doing further damage. This allows our immune and other underlying systems (for example, the heart, liver, brain, etc.) to go back to protecting our bodies from truly invasive threats.

Reaching for support accomplishes this. It shuts off the various physical and chemical processes that work to destroy our health, giving us back our cortex (the thinking brain) and allowing us to think through our problems. The brain then does its part once again in trying to help us correct the system. It signals the pituitary gland to secrete a powerful hormone called oxytocin.

According to Christopher Cardoso, researcher in Concordia's Center for Research in Human Development, "Previous studies have shown that natural oxytocin is higher in distressed people . . . In distressed people, oxytocin may improve one's motivation to reach out to others for support."[1] As a side benefit, it can help us heal. For example, in the heart, oxytocin can heal damaged cells and strengthen them. As this hormone secretes, it increases our desire to seek out others for comfort. It lowers the fear response and makes us more likely to want to trust, help, and be helped by others, which decreases fear even more. A brilliant cycle for supporting good health!

You might be wondering whether reaching for support to succeed in the area of physical health is something new. Actually, it was noted early on in our species' history because it was necessary for survival, once again due to our biology. As you may have noticed, the human body evolved to walk erect. To support the added weight in gravity, our pelvises became thicker, which left less room in the canal for infants to arrive. As a result, humans emerge from the womb less developed than almost any other mammal on Earth.

The need to protect and raise such vulnerable infants required us to develop considerable cooperation among adults. It became necessary to share food, for example, and hunting and gathering enough food to sustain groups, small or large, required the organized efforts of many. Reaching out to others allowed us to survive and, as a result, we have become accustomed to collaboration at a degree greater than any other species, including our primate cousins. Consider chimpanzees and gorillas, for example. They rarely let another mother hold their babies, unlike human mothers. In almost every culture studied, this is an acceptable behavior among humans and an extraordinary feat that we take for granted. As one author, Daniel Goleman, powerfully stated: ". . . to become a cooperatively breeding ape, and to persuade a bunch of smart, hot-tempered, suspicious, politically cunning primates to start sharing child care and provisioning, now that took a novel evolutionary development, the advent of this thing called trust."[2]

The necessity of reaching for support to insure survival across so many millennia seems to have created within us a persistent biological need to continue doing so, especially when we encounter fear. There is a tremendous amount of research that demonstrates the powerful effect of reaching for support on our physical health. These studies address health issues as varied as cardiac wellness, cancer, surgical and maternal outcomes, psychological health, and more. By sampling just a few of them, you'll begin to recognize how essential our connections with others are and how consistently they impact our physical health.

Most of us are generally aware that diet, exercise, and good sleep can affect the health of our heart, right? What may be less obvious, however, is that a willingness to reach for support can impact the heart just as powerfully as any other factor. Two brilliant cardiologists, Meyer Friedman and Ray Rosenman, referenced the importance of reaching out for support in their book, *Type A Behavior and Your Heart*. "Peculiarly," they wrote, "an anxiety state of severe degree—that is one in which the subject is profoundly depressed and seeks the help of others rather than relying upon his own possible powers for coping with his situation—is extraordinarily likely to reduce serum cholesterol to unusually low levels. This phenomenon has not been widely recognized."[3] It is believed that the mechanism for this physical improvement is that, when we reach for support and shut off the amygdala, the blood supply that it had been sending to the muscles returns to its normal flow, giving the liver the blood it needs to lower the cholesterol we feed it. If we re-read the previous quote and substitute the words *fear* for "anxiety" and *sad* for "depressed," we have strong evidence supporting the assertion that the most crucial skill for achieving and maintaining success in physical health is to reach out to others for support.

Additional cardiac studies have reached the same conclusions. Cardiologist Redford Williams, author of the book *Anger Kills*, followed 1,300 cardiac patients for five years after their initial diagnosis. He found that patients who were unmarried and reported that they had no one to confide in experienced a 50 percent death rate within five years. Those who were married or who indicated that they had someone to confide in, on the other hand, experienced only a 17 percent death rate. Similar findings were noted in older patients who were hospitalized with congestive heart failure. Those who said they had no one they could rely on for emotional support were three times more likely to have subsequent complications requiring re-hospitalization than those reporting that they had emotional support.[4] What these findings suggest is that reaching for support is an essential factor in improving and sustaining good heart health.

Surgical outcomes also improve when patients reach for and receive various types of support. One noteworthy study done by

James Kulik and Heike Mahler at the University of California, San Diego investigated whether or not one's roommate prior to heart surgery could have a meaningful impact on the outcome of this very technical procedure.[5] Half of the patients were assigned a roommate who was also scheduled for bypass surgery the following day, whereas the other half shared rooms with postoperative patients who were already successfully recovering from the same surgery. Which group do you predict had the best outcomes? If you guessed that having a recovering postsurgical roommate was most helpful, you are correct. The group of patients rooming with these "experienced mentors" ended up walking twice as far per day after the operation compared to those patients with preoperative roommates, and they were out of the hospital a full day and a half sooner.

Cardiac and surgical studies weren't the only ones to clearly demonstrate the importance of connection in achieving and sustaining health during medical challenges. Outcomes for women receiving support prenatally or when in labor have also been well-documented. One study that was reported in the *New England Journal of Medicine* followed 40 women who came into a hospital in labor alone, with no partner, parent, or friend accompanying them.[6] Half of the study participants, the control group, received the standard medical support routinely offered by the hospital. The other half, the experimental group, received "constant support from an untrained layperson from admission to delivery; one woman was present during the day and another at night. The support consisted of physical contact (for example, rubbing the mother's back and holding her hands), conversation, and the presence of a friendly companion whom the mother had not met before." The outcomes were telling. For the women in the control group, the average time from admission to delivery was 19.3 hours, whereas the average time from admission to delivery for the experimental group was only 8.7 hours.

In a similar maternal study, 465 first-time, healthy pregnant women were randomly assigned to one of two groups.[7] For the first group, it was arranged that a woman unacquainted with the soon-to-be mothers would come to the hospital to provide emotional support during labor and delivery. For the second group, the new mothers were scheduled to go through labor and delivery alone. Given what you now know about the importance of reaching for support, can you guess what the outcome was? As you might suspect, the group provided the supportive stranger fared best. They experienced fewer overall complications during labor, their labor time was halved, and fewer of their infants required intensive care after delivery. Additional maternal studies have reported a 60 percent reduction in pain medication and a 25 percent reduction in Caesarean sections when delivering mothers are provided support.

It has also been demonstrated that mutual, or simultaneous, support has a powerful effect on health habit changes and success with compliance as well. A study through the University College London followed 3,722 couples, all over age 50, who were either married or living together.[8] As might be expected, researchers found that when one partner was trying to make a change in his or her health behavior, that person was more likely to succeed if his or her partner was also making the change. What was most compelling in the findings, however, was the staggering difference in the rates of success. They found that if a woman was trying to quit smoking, she had a 50 percent chance of succeeding if her partner was also trying to quit, but had only an 8 percent chance if her partner remained a smoker.

Other important investigations have probed the *quality* of people's close relationships and the impact of this on a variety of physical health factors as well. Beginning in the 1950s, investigators randomly selected 126 Harvard undergraduates and asked them to answer a single question: "Would you describe your relationship to your mother and your father as (check one): *very close, warm and friendly, tolerant, strained and cold?*"[9] Thirty-five years later, the medical records of the 126 subjects were analyzed and findings were compared with their answers to this one question. The results were striking. Of those undergraduates who answered "strained and cold" regarding their relationship with the mother 35 years earlier, the chance of being diagnosed with a major medical problem such as heart disease or alcoholism was 90 percent, whereas of the study participants who had indicated that they were "very close to their mothers," only 45 percent had experienced a serious medical problem. For the students reporting distance from fathers, the risk of health problems was 82 percent compared to 50 percent for those with a warm relationship. Even more heartbreaking, for those students who answered "strained and cold" regarding their relationship with both parents, *the risk of severe illness was 100 percent!* A similar study was conducted at John Hopkins University in the 1940s in which 1,100 male medical students were also asked about their closeness to their fathers.[10] Their answers to this question turned out to be the best predictor of which subjects would develop cancer 50 years later. It was not thought that relationships with parent(s) prescribed destiny, but instead that subjects who could not reach out to their parents for support were unlikely to have created the loving, supportive relationships as adults that would prevent them from putting themselves at risk for health challenges.

Case Example

Sandra is a highly educated executive at a high tech firm in the Silicon Valley, with a jaw-dropping resume packed full of impressive accomplishments. Although she dates occasionally, she insists that she has no time in her life right now for a relationship. She came to see me looking for help with weight loss. "I keep gaining and losing the same 30 pounds," she remarked, a tinge of self-loathing and desperation evident in her voice. She said that it angered her that she could be so self-disciplined and successful at work, but could not control her eating and nutrition. It wasn't for lack of effort on her part, however. Sandra had repeatedly tried intensive exercise programs, restricted diets, and even medication. But, despite these efforts, the cycle of weight loss and gain persisted.

As we began to explore her pattern of eating, it became apparent that Sandra was already aware that she was "a stress eater." When she was upset, she consoled herself with food; and when she was excited about a work success, she rewarded herself with food. I began our conversation by asking her if we could explore just a few aspects of her childhood. I approached this topic gingerly, because she had pointedly told me she had not wanted to see a psychologist "to talk for hours about her childhood." I promised her that I just wanted to understand a few aspects of her upbringing that might be influencing her relationship with food and she guardedly agreed.

I asked first whether she'd gone to her parents with her problems as a child. She quickly answered, "No. They were both so tired when they came home from work. I took care of my two younger sisters, and my parents always said, 'You're a smart girl, you can figure it out on your own.'" She added that her mother had always seemed depressed and she didn't want to burden her. From these circumstances, Sandra learned to be hard-working and self-reliant. These two qualities, no doubt, were tremendously helpful in the highly competitive, male-dominated world of high tech firms. I asked her if there was anyone that she currently confides in, shares her problems with, or calls with her successes. There was a long silence, then her eyes began to fill. "No . . . no one at all." A pause. "Not ever." She seemed surprised by the tears that fell slowly along her cheeks and wiped them away. "I do have a lot of friends . . . and I go out a lot," she asserted. Then, as if realizing it for the first time, "But no one knows me. Not really."

Sandra, like many successful people, had achieved excellence and rewards in her work by hard work and competitive skills. However, she'd grown up without much emotional support, so she wasn't conscious of the basic human need to truly connect with others. I pointed out how powerful this need was by reminding her of what children do when they have a nightmare and what parents do in response. I then added an example she might relate to more easily: "So, consider things from this perspective. You've mentioned that you have 30 people who report to you. If any one of them, or your whole team, are facing a really difficult problem with a customer, would you want them to make their best guess and act or consult you before taking action?" She didn't hesitate. "Of course I'd want my staff to bring the issues to me." I paused to let her consider her response, then asked: "And you would want them to do this so you could monitor their work and compliment them or criticize their plans?" She responded quickly, "Of course not! I'd just want to be available so they could talk through things, brainstorm, and know they weren't in it alone."

As she said this, she immediately noticed the contradiction between her desire to have her staff bring issues to her and her own fiercely guarded self-reliance. I quickly tried to connect this budding awareness with her concerns about eating before she could accuse me of wanting to blame everything on her parents. "So," I suggested, "Since the healthy response to doubt, uncertainty, and stress [I assumed she would prefer this familiar word to the term *fear*] is to ask for help, and you feel you have no permission or channel to do this, where do you go instead?" She smiled wryly at her awareness that food had become her friend and her source of comfort when she was upset or stressed.

With this fresh perspective, she was ready to take on her weight management challenges once again. The steps we designed may appear simple to you, but they weren't easy for her. We started with a phone call. Every time she felt like overeating, or when her food choices would not help her to achieve her goals, she would call my voice mail and leave a basic message, "Hi this is Sandra" and then hang up. That this was difficult for her may seem foolish. However, to Sandra's emotional brain, reaching out to another person for support was dangerous. So, protectively, she had walled off her basic human need for support. Simply calling someone before reaching for food was inviting the rejection she had feared as a child.

Sandra was surprised at how difficult this was as well. I explained to her the importance of working to reprogram the brain in very small increments in order to side-step her instinctive fears and achieve lasting progress. (If you're interested in how to design "small steps" for any challenge you might be facing, please see my book *One Small Step Can Change Your Life*, which provides specific information on this important strategy and its underlying rationale.) It took more than a month before this habit became consistent and easy for Sandra, but eventually it did.

At that point, we added another step. She continued to call, but her voice mails now included a short description about how she was feeling prior to using food for comfort or to mask her feelings. Opening up in this way was again a challenging task. However, we both noticed that it became easier for her much more quickly. After a few weeks, with Sandra's habit of reaching out firmly established, we started developing an inventory of her friends and acquaintances. We looked through the list to carefully identify individuals she knew who were nurturing and supportive. We then role-played how Sandra might share various life challenges and successes, as well as her difficulty in opening up to others, with those friends. In this way, her fears of leaning on another person could become a bridge for connection rather than a wall.

Initially, Sandra selected one friend to reach out to—and she chose well. She asked this friend if they could connect more often to share successes and challenges, and she found that her friend was more than just willing, she was interested in growing the friend-ship as well. Although Sandra still had more work to do in order to achieve her weight-management goals, through this initial process her underlying relationship with food, along with her fundamental sense of herself in connection to others, was changed forever.

Sandra's situation addresses one specific health challenge. However, the approach reflects the important principles that underlie success in *any* health challenge. In order to achieve and sustain excellence in health, it is critical that we take three steps: 1) become aware of our own willingness to reach for support, or our fear of doing so; 2) identify people we can reach out to who will support us in achieving our health goals; and 3) reach out.

CHAPTER 6

Work Success

My model for business is the Beatles. They were four guys who kept each other's kind of negative tendencies in check. They balanced each other and the total was greater than the sum of the parts. That's how I see business: great things in business are never done by one person, they're done by a team of people.

—Steve Jobs

The Wealth in "We"

At no time in the business world do we more readily recognize the value of the word "we" than in those moments when everything is about to fall apart. Take, for example, a routine flight in February, 1989 that suddenly became anything but routine. United Airlines Flight 811 departed from the Honolulu Airport as usual, but within minutes of takeoff, a forward cargo door blew out, creating a gaping hole in the side of the aircraft. A portion of the cabin floor caved in, 10 seats were ejected from the plane, and nine passengers lost their lives. The reason that the plane, the crew, and the remaining passengers survived, according to Captain David Cronin, was the training he and his team had received called "command leadership resource management." In this extensive course, airline captains are taught to ask the copilot for input in emergency situations, and copilots are advised to challenge any decisions that they believe to be incorrect. The nightmare on board Flight 811 lasted less than 25 minutes, and during those minutes, the captain and first officer conferred steadily and debated strategy. In more than one instance, Captain Cronin agreed that the first officer's suggestion was on target and their shared decision-making led to the safe landing of the stricken plane. As Captain Cronin, a United Airlines veteran with 35 years of flying experience said, "In the old days, the other crew members didn't speak or do a thing until the captain told them to. Those days are now over."[1] Problem solving in businesses is a team sport. No one wins unless every player is doing his or her part.

Although many people appear to recognize the value of collaboration in business, there persists a common belief that there are certain men and women who accomplish great feats and achieve success in business on their own. Although this may occasionally be true, more often successful individuals have had enormous help along that way. Unfortunately, this doesn't always survive a later recounting.

> *A hundred times every day, I remind myself that my inner and outer life depends on the labor of other men, living and dead, and that I must exert myself in order to give in the measure as I have received and am still receiving.*
>
> —Albert Einstein

I first began to mull over this idea in greater depth while reading a book called *The Winner Within*, written by one of the greatest basketball coaches in NBA history, Pat Riley. Of course, anything Coach Riley has to teach about excellence is certainly worth a serious look. However, there was one sentence in the book that I thought was quite mistaken. The statement read, "It is much harder to truly act alone and succeed today in the way that entrepreneurs such as Thomas Edison or Henry Ford did in times past."[2]

In order to help you understand my perspective on this, let's take a brief look at the journeys that Edison and Ford took on their paths to business success. To begin with, Thomas Edison did not *invent* the light bulb. He was actually working under one as he struggled to improve it. As a result, when he applied for his first patent, it was rejected because the light bulb had already been patented! What Edison did accomplish, however, was nothing less than genius. He improved on the work of others. He reached out to those who had achieved past success and built on their work.

On his 80th birthday, Edison was asked which of his inventions made him most proud. An interesting question for someone who held over 1,000 U.S. patents at the time! He responded, "The use of the team in the laboratory." Edison worked with a total of 14 collaborators and, when his lab disbanded, he never invented again. His assistant, Francis Jehl, remarked, "Edison is, in reality, a collective noun and means the work of many men."[3]

When Henry Ford decided that he wanted to build automobiles, there were close to 100 manufacturers who were already building the machines, all by hand. Recognizing the extensive challenges, at one point Ford contemplated quitting. However, the woman he called his "true believer" (later to become his wife) convinced him to persist. So Ford went to work with his mentor, Thomas Edison, who talked him out of building an electric car and instead to encouraged him to build a gas-powered engine (you can decide how you feel about that!). Ford was making little progress until an observation in a meat packing plant in Chicago provided the inspiration needed to revolutionize the world of car manufacturing. Bill Klan, a junior mechanic in Ford's employ, watched butchers as they disassembled a carcass, with one butcher cutting off the breast, another the thigh, another the rump. Observing this, Klan foresaw its potential in building cars. Armed with this new inspiration, he approached Ford and together they decided that, if meat packers could disassemble a carcass in one direction, it was entirely possible that Ford and his team could build a car with a line going in the other direction. With this mix of support and collaboration among numerous people, the automotive assembly line was born.

Henry Ford and Thomas Edison were not isolated creative geniuses. They were more than that. They were brilliant collaborators who never stopped looking for new ideas and asking for help all along their paths to success. Not only did they actively seek out support, but they perceived doing so as a strength rather than a sign of weakness.

Although reaching for support may have seemed to come naturally to these inventors, others may not always find this easy to do. Take cardiac surgeons, for example. These medical professionals are often perceived as stoic and independent—possibly very necessary character traits to have when you literally have patients' lives in your hands on a daily basis! However, one group of these surgeons at the Mayo Clinic speculated that by working together, they may be able to cut costs and improve quality of care for their patients. With this in mind, they began a broad-scale comparison of how they were using blood transfusions in their work. After sharing perspectives and discovering important differences, they negotiated and created a standard protocol for use with various types of patients. Within a year, they'd reduced transfusions by 50 percent and reduced the risk of transfusion-related kidney disease by 40 percent. During the course of three years, they saved the Mayo Clinic $15 million dollars![4]

Research on the effect of teams on surgical success rates makes an even more dramatic case for the power of support in achieving successful results. For example, a study completed by Huckman and Pisano examined the success rate of 203 cardiac surgeons who conducted a total of more than 38,000 heart surgeries.[5] To clearly identify which factors most influenced the success of the surgeries, researches focused on a single type—coronary artery bypass grafts. When the data was analyzed, the findings were clear. The major predictor of surgical success was not how many of these operations a surgeon had performed in the past, but instead, the number of these surgeries that he or she had performed at a specific hospital. Although many of the surgeons operated at more than one hospital, investigators found that the majority were most successful at the hospital where they completed the most procedures. This was attributed to the effectiveness of the surgical team. When a surgeon operated frequently with the same group of nurses and surgical technicians, they all had an opportunity to learn one another's strengths and weaknesses. As a result, they discovered how to work together most effectively. In the end, it was the team that made the surgeon and outcomes successful.

The effect of teams on the performance of individual "stars" has been noted across many other professions as well. Take, for example, the wizards of the financial world. Boris Groysberg, Professor of Business Administration at Harvard Medical School, followed the careers of 366 "star analysts" across multiple investment firms.[6] These were high performers whose clients prospered under their guidance. What made these analysts the object of Groysberg's study, however, was that they each took their fame and fortune and moved to another firm. Following the transition, most of them failed to maintain their exceptional results and the firms who hired them lost millions. There was one small group of star analysts, however, who sustained their status. These were the ones who took their teams with them. What made these people "stars" was not simply their own individual talents, but their ability to create and sustain high-functioning teams who could help them in accomplishing exceptional goals. In these new settings, having immediate access to well-cultivated relationships and professional support in achieving their goals was especially advantageous.

It is not just routine for thriving individuals and organizations to have rich, plentiful support systems (we're speaking in terms of quality of course), but also for them to see asking for and receiving support as a sign of strength. Consider, for example, the success of Disney's Pixar Animation Studios. Ed Catmull, President of Disney Animation and CEO of Pixar, was first and foremost a dreamer. When he achieved his PhD in computer science, he envisioned making full-length, animated movies using the newest technologies. His dream had no chance of reaching fruition, however, until he caught the attention of film producer George Lucas, who hired Catmull to reap the benefits of his technological skill and artistic vision. Seven years later, with the vision and financial support of Steve Jobs backing him (Pixar would have gone bankrupt long before completion without Jobs), Catmull hired a talented animator named John Lassiter who had been previously fired by Disney Studios. With support from all sides, Catmull and his team developed the technology and animated films that fulfilled his dreams.

Lassiter, who today is the Chief Creative Officer at Pixar, is undeniably a genius as well. Like Catmull, he recognizes his genius as only one part in the amazing success of Pixar. Notice how Lassiter describes their process for achieving success, especially how often the word "we" shows up: "Because *we* are a culture of inventors, nothing is standard operating procedure for us. *We* constantly reevaluate and re-examine everything *we* do. *We* go back and study what works and what didn't work, and *we* get excited about what didn't work because, for us, that's a challenging new problem to solve."[7] Catmull, too, has described how essential it is to build supportive relationships in organizations: "Of great importance—and something that sets us apart from other studios—is the way people at all levels support one another. Everyone is fully invested in helping everyone else turn out the best work. They really do feel that it's all for one and one for all."[8]

Seeking allies in the workplace often requires imagination. Consider the birth of Arthur Fry's Post-it notes. What now seems like an obvious success story was originally met with little enthusiasm at 3M when it was first invented. In fact, his supervisors rejected it. Not to be deterred, Fry reached for support to an unusual source. He gave his bosses' secretaries Post-it notes to use in their daily work and then, months later, informed them that the product was no longer available. By that time, of course, they had already discovered the immense value of the product and they prevailed on their bosses to reverse the decision. From there, the Post-it became one of the most successful products 3M has ever launched!

Successful collaboration sometimes defies traditional barriers. Reaching for support may occur not only within organizations, but between them as well. Toyota is famous for this unusual type of collaboration. For example, they go out of their way to teach quality control, share proprietary information, and build life-long relationships with not only their employees, but their suppliers as well. This perspective may have been developed when the company was rebuilding out of the rubble of World War II and they were dependent on, and vulnerable to, their suppliers for their continued existence. They worked diligently to create trusting, dependable relationships. Toyota still views their suppliers as part of their support system today—they strive to be loyal and expect loyalty among all their connected organizations.

We do not just build cars, we build people.

—Toyota

Automobile companies in the United States, on the other hand, tend more often to treat suppliers as competitors. They may pit one against the other when trying to get the cheapest price possible. An article in the *Harvard Business Review* described the differences between Toyota and American car companies' relationships with their suppliers this way:

It (Toyota) treats key suppliers as long-term partners, shares development work with them, and sticks with them over the long term. When a Toyota supplier is struggling, Toyota sends in its own people to help. In sharp contrast, U.S. auto companies have generally treated their suppliers as adversaries. They keep them on a tight leash. They typically offer them short contracts and all too often base their purchasing decisions largely on price. When a supplier has a problem, the U.S. auto company's typical response has been to terminate the contract.[9]

Toyota's reign as the largest and most profitable car company in the world may be due, in part, to their philosophy of embracing supporters outside of traditional barriers.

Recognition of the need for collaboration and mentorship in business is not a new idea. The mentorship necessary to build and fully master a skill or trade, in fact, was provided systematically in the practice of apprenticeship, which was epitomized by the guilds that flourished in the 1400s in Florence, Italy. If parents wished their child to become a painter, a weaver, or a goldsmith, the child was sent by the age of seven to live with a master crafts-man for a period of up to 10 years. Daniel Coyle described this process in his book *The Talent Code*:

> An apprentice worked directly under the tutelage and supervision of the master, who frequently assumed rights as the child's legal guardian. Apprentices learned the craft from the bottom up, not through lecture or theory, but through action: mixing paint, preparing canvasses, sharp-ening chisels. They cooperated and competed within a hierarchy, rising after some years to the status of a journey-man and, eventually, if they were skilled enough, a mas-ter. This system created a chain of mentoring. Da Vinci studied under Verrocchio, Verrocchio under Donatello, Donatello under Ghiberti, Ghiberti under Baldovinetti, and so on. All of them frequently visited one another's studios in a cooperative, competitive arrangement that today would be called social networking.[10]

Although a return to apprenticeships in business today may not be practical, the idea of mentorship remains invaluable not only in the business world, but in many other areas of life as well. Reaching for support by observing others, collaborating with them, and seeking out mentors who can help you to develop your knowledge and skills or your products and services are critical for long-term business success.

Giving Support

So far, we have focused primarily on identifying your needs and developing the courage to ask for the help. As you begin to reach out for support in the business world, however, you will quickly discover that the other half of this essential skill is to be able to give help to others when it is needed. For any organization, team, or individual to succeed in the workplace, it is not only essential that team members be willing to ask for support, but they must also be invested in giving support to those in need. Some enlightening research on the importance of this is captured in Adam Grant's book, *Give and Take*.[11] Early in the book, he asks a compelling question that I will now ask you: *Do you think givers are the most productive, most successful employees in an organization, or are they the least productive, least successful members?*

The surprising answer is "yes!" Both are correct. Givers tend to migrate both to the top and the bottom on a scale of successful employees. What is the primary difference between those who are most and least successful? Givers who thrive are those who are able to set limits on what they will give to whom, and when, so that they are not giving beyond their capacity at their own expense. Givers who find it challenging to set limits often help others at the cost of getting their own work completed or goals realized.

Analyzing the comparative values of giving and taking in the workplace becomes even more complicated when the data is mined further. In a study of medical students' school performance, for example, it was discovered that the students most generous with their time and resources were generally less successful overall in terms of grades during their first years.[12] However, as training continued, the givers became the most successful students in the class. What do you believe might underlie these findings? A look at the learning structure may provide the answer. During the first two years of medical training, classroom education, studying for and taking tests, and competing against other students for recognition by professors are primary areas of focus. During these years, the givers helped others to study and they shared their resources. After that early period, the remainder of a medical student's educational training (and their subsequent medical practice) is dependent on working with others—cooperating, collaborating, and putting patients' interests ahead of getting credit for work or being more compelling than other students.

Reid Hoffman, founder of LinkedIn, provides an excellent summary of the powerful effects of giving support in the workplace: "It seems counterintuitive, but the more altruistic your attitude, the more benefits you will gain from the relationship. If you set out to help others, you will rapidly reinforce your own reputation and expand your universe of possibilities."[13] Francis Flynn, in a research project reported in the *Academy of Management Journal*, reiterated this after investigating the productivity levels of a group of telecommunication engineers. He discovered that the most successful engineers, as measured by both productivity level and respect among peers, were the ones who gave generously to others and helped others the most—they recognized that asking for help was essential and they rewarded other staff for reaching out.[14]

The impact of giving, of providing support in the workplace was also evident in the findings of a study conducted by Google, who set out to investigate their best and worst managers. Laszlo Bock, Senior Vice President, described the initiation of the research as follows: "The starting point was that our best managers have teams that perform better, are happier—they do everything better. So the biggest controllable factor we could see was the quality of the manager, and how they made things happen." During the study, they collected over 10,000 observations. What they culled from the research they termed "the eight skills of the best managers." Bock said, "In the Google context, we'd always believed that to be a manager, particularly on the engineering side, you need to be as deep or deeper of a technical expert than the people who work for you. It turns out that's absolutely the least important thing. It's important, but pales in comparison."[15] What they discovered, in fact, was that the best managers—those with the most productive teams—were doing three things. They were meeting often with their employees, they showed an interest in people's personal lives, and they asked many questions rather than just giving commands or instructions. What this suggests is that providing support to your team is not just a nice thing to do, but an essential component in building organizational success.

Following is a brief exercise to help you as you begin to become more aware of your skills in this area of giving support to others:

Consider the following questions:

1. Do you believe that givers or takers are more productive and successful in your work setting? In your organization, which colleagues and managers do you see as givers and takers?
2. Do you consider yourself a giver, a taker, or both?
3. Are givers in your organization able to set limits on giving?
4. If you are in management, do you meet frequently with your team, ask many questions, and show an interest in people's personal lives?

In addition to improving outcomes for organizations, giving support has surprising health benefits that rival the benefits of reaching out and asking for help. One rather dramatic study illustrating this followed the lives of 846 adult men and women in Detroit during a five-year span. At the start of the study, all of the subjects listed how many stressful events had occurred in their lives during the previous year. They were also asked to estimate how much time they spent supporting others in their community. Five years later, when researchers looked at how many of the 846 were alive, they found that the subjects who reported very little giving to others were 30 percent more likely to have already died compared to the givers.[16]

Work Stress

One of the most intriguing studies of workplace stress was undertaken in the 1970s and 1980s at the Illinois Bell Phone Company. Two researchers, Salvatore Maddi and Suzanne Kobasa, chose a high-stress group of executives (mid- and upper-level executives) to follow during the time when the monopoly that Bell had enjoyed for a period of time was at an end. All subjects were male, a somewhat typical distribution at that time, and the occupations of the executives included a wide variety of professionals, including accountants, lawyers, financial analysts, engineers, sales supervisors, and others. The study question was, "How would each of these leaders fare when all the rules changed?"[17] During the eight years of the study, each executive was contacted a minimum of five times for participation in intensive interviews. Questions asked probed descriptions of the managers' physical states and their attitudes toward the huge professional challenges they were facing.

The interviews were extensive. As several of the interviewers described the process: "We got information about not only our executives' stressful life events, but also factors of personality, social supports, coping efforts, health practices, constitutional strengths and weaknesses (assessed through family medical histories), and physiological functioning. Data on physiological functioning and constitutional status came from medical examinations."

Findings from the project revealed that the external stress of the upheaval at work did not explain nor predict an executive's work performance or physical health. Instead, the executive's *attitude* was the factor that was highly predictive. From the data, researchers identified "The Three Cs"—commitment, control, and challenge. Hardy executives felt a *commitment* to their work and to their families. They felt optimistic that they could gain *control* of difficult situations, and they tended to perceive these difficult situations as an exciting *challenge.*

To achieve and maintain these three Cs, social support was perceived as crucial. By "support" the researchers were referring not only other people at work, but also each manager's childhood experiences in being able to reach for and receive support. Findings of the study suggested that the development of "hardiness" was a direct result of the executives' experiences in childhood. The parents of successful executives were described as supportiv and accepting, showing interest and encouragement. Less hardy executives, those who had developed physical and performance problems, had parents who were frequently described as "hostile, disapproving, or neglectful." What the research revealed was that having nurturing parents in childhood provided many of these executives, decades later, with important tools for mastering life's challenges.

Regarding support in the workplace, the authors noted: "In coping transformationally, it helps to have the warm appreciation, encouragement, admiration, and goodwill of other people around you. But, in addition to encouragement and goodwill, there is another aspect of social support that can increase transformational coping: the know-how and resources that come from associating with capable people engaged in efforts similar to your own." The authors were very clear about the fact that having someone who merely sympathized with a person's frustrations and agreed that life was difficult would not be helpful. They stated, "Only the kind of support that encourages someone to appraise stressful events optimistically and act decisively to change them qualifies as a resistance resource." Resistant resources describe any tool an executive used to stay physically healthy and effective in the workplace. This now famous research made the powerful case that it is not stress (fear) itself that determines our outcomes both physically and vocationally, but rather the types of support we have available to us and our skill in addressing it.

Hiring Practices

Assessing potential employees to determine whether or not they possess the critical skill of asking for and giving support is not always easy. In my work as a business consultant, I have found two strategies that seem to work particularly well in accomplishing this. Not long ago, I was interviewing the CEO of one of the largest companies in Europe and I asked him how he goes about choosing his key employees. I was somewhat surprised when he said, "I ask them only one question." Puzzled, I asked him what it was. He said, "By the time the candidate gets to me, their technical competence has been determined. So I simply ask them, 'Please tell me one accomplishment you are proud of.'" This answer did not satisfy my curiosity. "If they are good enough to have made it to an interview with you," I said, "then they must have a very long list of accomplishments. What are you listening for?" His answer made perfect sense. "I don't listen to the whole sentence, just the first word. Does the candidate start the sentence with 'I' or 'we'? If they think they can accomplish anything in life on their own, they are a fool, and I don't want fools working for me."

In another instance, I was consulting with management staff for an airline that was interviewing flight attendant applicants. The process they used to achieve hiring success was unique. They would ask four or five applicants to come into a room and sit on chairs circling each other. They then asked each applicant to stand and give a short speech on why he or she wanted to work for the airline. Skeptical about this approach, I asked, "What's your reason for doing this? The job doesn't typically involve public speaking—the only flight attendant giving passengers instructions is reading from a script." The interviewer's response was much wiser than my question:

We don't really listen to what the person who is standing is saying. We watch what the other applicants are doing. Are they keeping eye contact, nodding at the correct moments, looking away, or looking at their watch? What we want to know is, what they will do under duress? We want to be certain that if a fellow flight attendant is at the back of the plane dealing with an unruly passenger, the applicant is someone who will come to help rather than find some excuse to stay in the front galley.

When interviewing candidates for important positions, many successful organizations reach out to staff at all levels for help in determining who might be the best fit. Southwest Airlines, for example, is proud of its approach in selecting employees who have the potential to work well together at all levels. In fact, I have over-heard two of their past CEOs tell the exact same story with great satisfaction. Southwest had just completed interviews and was pre-paring to hire a new pilot. However, one of the secretaries who had taken his phone calls during the interview-scheduling process stated that this pilot had been rude to her on more than one occasion. That one piece of information from one office staff person was enough to doom the pilot's entire career at Southwest Airlines.

Whole Foods, another undeniably successful organization, demonstrates similar care in consulting relevant team members before hiring. They do not hire new employees until the staff in the new hire's intended department has vetted them. Team members evaluate them to decide if they will stay. This sort of multi-level collaboration achieves two important goals. First, the process helps to decrease fear. Not only do staff members at all levels get to know a potential hire, but they also feel that their input is valued. Each of these factors reduces fear in the hiring process. Second, and in turn, management receives valuable input, an essential form of support, from those most critical in assuring the hire's success.

Rewarding Support

Successful organizations not only reach to their employees for sup-port and encourage staff to reach out to one another, but they also find creative ways to reward employees who support the organization or fellow employees. Take Enterprise, for example, one of the largest rental car companies in the United States. Enterprise has four main criteria that they use to assess a manager's suitability for promotion. The first is customer satisfaction; the second is branch growth; the third is branch profitability; and the fourth is "the number of promotable management candidates developed at the branch." This fourth measure is especially important. It encourages managers to view their staff members as protégés, people to be mentored. When we stop to consider this, we realize that mentoring and developing others is essential to achieving success in all the other areas as well!

Reducing Error

Every organization strives toward perfection, but "high reliability organizations" (HROs) do more than just strive. They must actually achieve near perfection or lives will be lost. HROs are organizations such as aircraft carriers, nuclear power plants, and hospital emergency departments—workplaces where team efforts may cause or prevent injury or death. These types of organizations were extensively studied by Dr. Karl Weick and his findings are reported in the book *Managing the Unexpected*. Weick discovered that there are two organizational skills essential for achieving a workplace as close to perfection as we humans are capable of realizing. The first is that companies and managers must pay close attention to mistakes while they are so small that they do not appear to be particularly important. The second is that the organizations must make it safe for employees to bring their doubts or slip-ups to management without fear of punishment. He described the overlap between these two essential factors as follows:

HROs are aware of the close tie between sensitivity to operations and sensitivity to relationships. People who refuse to speak up out of fear enact a system that knows less than it needs to know to remain effective. People in HROs know that you can't develop a big picture of operations if the symptoms of those operations are withheld. It makes no difference whether they are withheld out of fear, ignorance, or indifference. All those reasons for withholding tend to be relational . . . people need to feel safe to report incidents or they will ignore them or cover them up. Managerial actions such as encouraging questions and rewarding people who report errors or concerns can strengthen an organization wide culture that values reporting.[18]

In one study supporting this contention, investigators examined the number of errors occurring on hospital nursing units and analyzed these in relationship to the perceived confidence nurses had that reporting them would lead to system improvements rather than punishment. Initially, those units where nurses felt safest had the most reported errors. However, across time, those same units experienced the least number of mistakes. Researchers concluded that the freedom to report challenging issues and mistakes led to solutions and fewer mistakes, whereas on the less safe nursing units, mistakes were ignored or hidden and, so, grew with time.[19]

It is utterly impossible to achieve success without making mistakes along the way. Organizations that recognize this fact and encourage employees to share their mistakes when they are still small tend to reduce errors and reap large long-term rewards. Although Toyota may not be considered an HRO, the organization is famous for creating a safe environment and encouraging front-line employees to bring problems to management immediately. To achieve rapid communication of problems, they have used the Andon Cord system, an emergency cable strung above assembly lines. This has come to symbolize the built-in quality of the Toyota Way.[20] When an assembly line staff notices any problem, large or small, that person pulls the cord to summon managers and others to fix the problem immediately, before the customer is the one to discover it. The Andon Cord is symbolic of the partnership Toyota fosters between labor and management and a proven way to increase workers' perception of safety in reporting mistakes. (Note: In 2014, this was replaced with a yellow call button, which maintains this model of efficiency.)

As previously mentioned, it is impossible to achieve success without making mistakes along the way. This obvious fact raises two questions: First, when you make a mistake are you curious about it or critical of yourself? Second, in your organization, is it safe for people to ask for help and admit mistakes without fear of punishment? In Chapter 9, we will discuss how to "reprogram" the brain so you can stay curious and compassionate in the face of mistakes. In the meantime, if you are in a leadership position, consider these questions: How do you make it safe for your people to bring their mistakes to you? Do your team members feel free to bring their questions, concerns, and mistakes to you and your organization? As you explore this thought further, you may want to consider asking some of your key employees to share their perceptions in this regard.

Systems for Support

Successful leaders recognize that they play an important role in their companies but, more importantly, they appreciate that they share in the success of the whole organization. For this reason, many companies have worked hard to build in rituals for support traveling in both directions. Recall, for example, how the best airlines train their pilots in crew resource management strategies, advising the captain to ask for help when doubtful and encouraging the first officer to challenge decisions that do not appear to be safe. There are other professions, quite diverse, that would benefit from building stronger support protocols as well. The field of education may provide us with a good example. Turnover in American education is high, averaging 40 to 50 percent in five years. Novice teachers are frequently left alone to develop their skills with little assistance from mentors. In Japan, however, the turnover is much less. There, they employ a technique called *jugyokenkyu*, which means "lesson study." In this model, senior teachers sit in on one another's classes and provide detailed feedback regarding the successes and opportunities noted. In most advanced countries, many of which have students who consistently outperform students in the United States on tests, more time is provided outside of the classroom for teachers to help one another develop additional skills. One critic of American teacher education wrote: "Teaching is all consuming, and that absorption is part of the joy of the job. But if teaching is to be a profession of the mind (as well as of the heart) that retains top talent and delivers results on the same level that other countries boast, the people who spend hours with our children in the classroom also need what they currently don't get: the hours with peers and mentors that are essential to improving their craft."[21] Organizations who want their people to succeed make it a priority to develop systems for employee support.

One dramatic example of the value of providing systems of support comes from a General Motors factory in Fremont, California.[22] The factory opened in 1963 and, before long, it became one of the worst-performing factories in the General Motors system. Absenteeism, substance abuse, low productivity, and even lower quality were the norm. Labor-management strife was ongoing and GM closed the factory with some relief in 1982. Then, in 1983, Toyota and General Motors struck up a deal for a very strange partnership. Toyota agreed to build GM cars in Fremont using Toyota management techniques and GM's parts and design. Why, you might ask, would such an odd coupling occur? GM was eager to learn Toyota's strategies for building high quality cars and Toyota wanted to reduce trade friction with the U.S. and determine whether or not they could effectively export their management system and sustain their high quality with an American work force. Reluctantly, Toyota took back all of the employees that GM had found so difficult. But the changed system worked—dramatically so. Absenteeism and substance abuse stopped, productivity was twice what it had been, and the quality was the highest of any GM factory in the world. Even better, the turnaround took only two years.

So what did Toyota do to accomplish this? In addition to the Andon Cord, they provided a system of support that empowered workers. Managers at the old GM plant had walked the floor, telling workers what they should and shouldn't be doing. The Toyota-trained managers, on the other hand, believed that their role was to support the ideas and suggestions of the workers. A new system was put into place and staff were trained to help and critique one another. As reported in *Economic Perspectives*:

> Toyota divided the workforce into 350 teams, each consisting of five to seven people and a team leader. All workers had been taught techniques for describing and analyzing physical tasks. Team members design all the team's jobs, time each other with stopwatches, and explore ways of improving their own performance. They then compare their results with those of the other shift at the same workstation. This process goes on continually. Team members are trained to do each other's jobs and regularly rotate tasks among themselves.[23]

Healthy Employees

After reading the last chapter, I hope that you are completely convinced that relationships, and the ability to reach for support, have far-reaching effects on our health. A powerful example of this was demonstrated in a study focusing on the work life of traffic enforcement officers (sometimes referred to as "meter maids"). Now, it doesn't take much imagination to envision how incredibly stressful (fearful) this sort of job might be. Dr. Elizabeth Brondolo studied the stress response in 70 of these officers in New York City.[24] For this investigation, the subjects were asked to wear portable blood pressure devices to monitor their physical arousal (stress) throughout their workday. Findings revealed that both male and female traffic enforcement officers experienced better health responses when they perceived support in their work environment. Even in the presence of irate automobile owners, women officers who described their supervisors as supportive presented dramatically lower blood pressures compared to those who did not perceive this sort of support. For male officers, describing their fellow officers as supportive was the best predictor of low blood pressure on difficult days. What these findings suggest is that a person's *perception* of support can have a significant effect on employee health as well.

Conflict: An Essential Ingredient

It's far better to learn about problems from colleagues when there's still time to fix them than from the audience after it is too late.

—Ed Catmull, President, Pixar
Studios and Disney Animation

Recall from our earlier discussion that one vital component in all supportive relationships is "rejection," which includes giving and receiving meaningful feedback. Ed Catmull devoted much of his insightful book, *Creativity, Inc.*, to describing exactly how a leader can make an environment safe enough so that team members feel able to constructively criticize one another's ideas, accept critical feedback, and achieve positive results.[25] One of Catmull's first tasks after assuming leadership of Disney Animation was to teach writers and animators how to effectively give and receive critical feedback. He believed, as do most successful leaders, that disagreement is an essential component in achieving success.

The first rule in decision-making is that one does not make a decision unless there is disagreement.
—Peter Drucker

Constructing collaborative teams is a complex enterprise. Creating a safe environment for individuals to admit ignorance, ask for guidance, and develop trust among employees to a level where people feel free to disagree is an even more difficult task. Putting people together who know each other well can make this even more complicated, because teams who have long-established, trusting relationships may be especially hesitant to disagree with one another. They may put the comfort of their relationships ahead of the need to engage in conflict. This was well-illustrated in an experiment conducted by Brian Uzzi at Northwestern University, who was seeking to identify the ideal team composition to maximize creativity. To explore this factor, Uzzi investigated the teams that come together to produce Broadway plays. These teams are, by necessity, multidisciplinary. They involve artists with a variety of skills such as music, acting, choreography, and set design, as well as business professionals like those in marketing, finance, etc. Both artistically and commercially, Uzzi sought to discover what *quality* of relationships led to the most successful outcomes. His question was, "Do teams that have worked together in the past create better results than teams with no familiar members?" To answer this question, Uzzi examined the team composition of every Broadway musical between 1945 and 1989, which included 474 plays—a worthy sample!

What he discovered was that, because theatre is comprised of a relatively small community, there is much overlap from one play to the next. In an article in *The New Yorker,* Jonah Lehrer summarized Uzzi's intriguing findings: "Uzzi devised a way to quantify the density of these connections, a figure he called Q. If musicals were being developed by teams of artists who had worked together several times before—a common practice, because Broadway producers see 'incumbent teams' as less risky—those musicals would have an extremely high Q. A musical created by a team of strangers would have a low Q."[26]

According to the data, relationships among collaborators emerged as a reliable predictor of Broadway success. If the Q score was too low, say a 1.7 on a 5 point scale, the failure rate was high. These findings were expected. What was surprising, however, was that if the Q score was too high, above 3.2, productions also had a high failure rate. If people worked together too many times, they grew too close and comfortable with one another and creativity suffered. The "bliss point," as Uzzi called it, was a score of between 2.4 and 2.6. Teams with these scores were three times more likely to succeed compared to those with low or high Q scores. Lehrer's article quotes Uzzi's description of the "bliss point teams." He writes: "The best Broadway teams, by far, were those with a mix of relationships. These teams had some old friends but they also had newbies. The mixture meant that the artists could interact efficiently—they had a familiar structure to fall back on, but they also managed to incorporate some new ideas. They were comfortable with each other, but they weren't too comfortable."

So, are the most creative teams composed of people who consider one another friends? The answer to this is both yes and no. Friendship can encourage or impede people's tendencies to the reach for critical support. A study of team performance conducted by Joe Labianca and colleagues at Yonsei and Hansung University also explored the effects of friendship among team members.[27] They investigated the effectiveness of 60 teams at 11 companies across a variety of industries. What they discovered, similar to Uzzi's findings, was that wholesale congeniality can make teams less effective. In this study, the most effective teams were comprised of at least 50 percent members who considered each other friends. However, as the percentage of team members who considered themselves friends approached 100 percent, their performance dropped dramatically. The authors summarized, "Such groups suffer because they are insular, impermeable to outside influences, and unhealthily self-reliant." They stated that the friendships that benefit these teams the most are formed outside of the group. By interacting with managers and staff in other departments, group members are able to bring back to their groups strategic information, task-related advice, and political and social support that help groups to achieve success. The authors suggested that, as the number of friends in a business group increases, it's important for management to recognize the risks and appoint as least one member to act as "devil's advocate" who can look for flaws and share concerns regarding team decisions.

When encouraging conflict, it is also essential to establish an environment that supports successful resolutions. One of the most critical skills in conflict resolution is the ability to maintain curiosity about the other person or position, demonstrating respect for their perspectives and needs. We explored this idea earlier in the gourmet guide (Chapter 4). When there are heated emotions around the table, asking questions is often not easy. However, numerous studies support the value of making inquiries and showing interest in and understanding of one's opponents in order to achieve business success. In a nine-year study comparing "excellent" vs. "average" business negotiators, for example, negotiations were taped and then evaluated. Not surprisingly, it was discovered that the outstanding negotiators spent twice as much time asking questions compared to average negotiators.[28]

It is not only the ability to ask good questions that underlies business success, but the willingness to state opinions as well—especially those outside of the status quo. One recent study investigated what the authors called "observable candor" in teams at large U.S. banking firms. Business consultant Keith Ferrazzi evaluated team performance at six banks, measuring the degree to which members were able to effectively disagree with one another. What he found was a direct correlation between the members' willingness to disagree and their individual performance at work during the recession of 2008 and in the years that followed.[29] In response to these findings, Ferrazzi offered three suggestions to enhance candor in the business environment. The first was to divide teams into smaller groups of two to three individuals for part of each meeting to brainstorm solutions. He had observed that in groups of five or more people, one or two individuals were likely to dominate the conversation. As a result, other members tended to fear disagreement. He next suggested that groups elect a "Yoda" (remember the wise character from the movie *Star Wars?*), whose role is to "notice and speak up when something is left unsaid." The "Yoda" is also tasked with providing feedback to people if their candor is not constructive or if it is rude. His final suggestion was that teams set rules or specific guidelines as to how candor is to be expressed. For example, rather than bluntly disagreeing, team members might introduce ideas with phrases such as "I wonder if . . ." or "Can I suggest another way of looking at this?" According to Ferrazzi, these steps tend to result in more successful, more effective teams.

Remember that not all conflict is bad. In fact, it is one of the most important types of support we can provide in business and it is a necessary component in achieving organizational success. What is most important is not *which* rules a team chooses for managing conflict, but that they *have* well-defined, consistent rules so that healthy conflict can occur and lead to better decision-making.

Summary

The successful person often discusses fear and support in the same breath. In an interview with the *New York Times*, Howard Schultz, CEO of Starbucks, was asked, "What advice would you give to somebody about to become a CEO?" He responded:

I would say the following: Very few people . . . get into that seat and believe that they are now qualified to be the CEO. So everyone you meet has a level of insecurity. The level of insecurity that you have is a strength, not a weakness. The question is, how are you going to use it? For whatever reason, people believe that when they get to that spot they have to know everything. They've got to be in total control and can never show weakness. I would say one of the underlying strengths of a great leader and a great CEO—not all the time, but when appropriate—is to demonstrate vulnerability, because that will bring people closer to you and show people the human side of you. In order to demonstrate vulnerability, you have to make sure you have people around who will never use that against you, because you trust them and they trust you. So the ability, behind closed doors, to have open and honest conversations with your team about the concerns you have, the *fears* you have, and the opportunities, is the balance one needs to succeed.[30]

My real talent is in picking people.

—Jerry Seinfeld

CHAPTER 7

Creativity

Myth Understandings

One of the most enduring myths in the creativity literature is the notion of the lone creator, the brilliant individual who has invented or discovered life-saving medicines, extraordinary consumer products, or great works of art. In reality, the most authoritative studies of creativity consistently report that the very opposite is true. Consider, for example, this summary of the research noted in John Briggs' excellent book, *Fire in the Crucible: The Alchemy of Creative Genius*: "The legend of the lone creator is wrong. In recent years, investigators have begun to appreciate that creators collaborate in all sorts of ways in order to do their work. In fact, collaboration is one of the best kept secrets in creativity."[1]

In the world of art, collaboration and reaching for support has always been the norm, even among artists whose work would, at first glance, appear to be a solo endeavor. As mentioned previously, Picasso and Braque painted side-by-side, collaborating and criticizing one another's work as they exchanged ideas across many years. In 1888, Van Gogh spent time at the side of Paul Gauguin, the two postimpressionists working and creating together. Their impact on one another's work was described by one author in the following way: "After parting ways, neither artist could escape the other's influence. Gauguin's work began to have more religious themes after being influenced by Van Gogh's strong religious background. Gauguin also began using brighter colors, especially yellow, and thicker brush strokes like Van Gogh. Van Gogh began to use Gauguin's technique of painting from memory. This caused his paintings to become more decorative and less realistic."[2]

Visual artists are just one example of many types of individuals whose work is improved by collaboration with others. We often think of writers as solitary creatures, generating creative energy out of their self-imposed isolation and growing ideas in the silent spaces around them. However, many notable writers candidly acknowledge the importance of collaborating with others in their field. For example, C.S. Lewis remarked that he could never have written *The Chronicles of Narnia* without the help of J.R.R. Tolkien. In turn, Tolkien said that he could never have completed *The Lord of the Rings* without the assistance of—guess who? C.S. Lewis of course![3]

Nothing new that is really interesting comes without collaboration.

—James Watson, co-discoverer of
the DNA Double Helix

Some of the world's most successful inventors in the arts, science, business, and media have benefited exceedingly from ongoing collaboration with a wide variety of individuals throughout their careers. Take Walt Disney, a name synonymous with creativity. He was responsible for bringing to life the most famous mouse in the world. This timeless creature, however, was not conceived by Disney alone. In fact, Disney had originally planned to call his pivotal character *Mortimer Mouse*. When he shared this with his wife, Lillian, she advised, "Not Mortimer, it's too formal. How about Mickey?"[4] And with this, the mouse we now all know and love came to be. There are two important points to highlight in this story. First, in his creative endeavors, Disney purposefully sought out a wide variety of people who could give him suggestions, advice, and new ideas. And second, he was willing to listen to and act on others' advice.

Like all successful inventors, Disney allowed his creativity to be continually inspired by others. As a result, his creative successes grew and expanded across time. His visit to a charming amusement park in Copenhagen, Denmark was the spark for his now worldwide Disney theme parks, and many of his other creative ventures were inspired in a similar manner as well. For instance, Disney is credited with inventing an enduring new art form—the full-length animated cartoon. How did Disney develop the idea for this? Like most creative people, he journeyed through each day looking about him for all that he could take in, learn from, and be inspired by. In this particular case, Disney had invited his wife on holiday in France. While walking along the streets of Paris one day, he turned a corner and noticed movie-goers waiting in line to watch a series of seven of Disney's short cartoons. His curiosity was piqued. He suspected that if people would pay to watch several short cartoons at one time, they might also be willing to pay to watch one long sketch. With that collaborative thought in mind, Disney went to work to create his first full-length feature. Carelessly dubbed "Walt's Folly" by the local newspapers, we came to know it as *Snow White.*

Breakthrough inventions and discoveries in any domain are also almost always the result of collaboration. Consider once again Steve Jobs of Apple computers. He was inspired to create the incredibly successful Mac computer after examining an early desktop model and crude mouse during a tour of Xerox's labs. Jobs later remarked, "What we saw was incomplete and flawed, but the germ of the idea was there . . . within ten minutes it was obvious to me that all computers would work like this."[5] Jobs' collaboration with others in this new creative endeavor did not end there. He reached out and hired 15 Xerox employees who had worked on various facets and phases of the early computers and he partnered with Steve Wozniak, an engineering wizard who possessed the skills necessary to construct the machines. In the end, of course, this reaching out resulted in incredible success.

Jobs views his reliance on others for creative support as a strength. In an interview for *Wired Magazine*, Jobs commented:

"Creativity is just connecting things. When you ask creative people how they did something, they feel a little guilty because they really didn't do it, they just *saw* something. It seemed obvious to them after a while. That's because they were able to connect experiences they've had and synthesize new things."[6] When Jobs returned to Apple, he persisted in developing powerful, collaborative alliances across time. For instance, he made a bargain with his arch competitor, Bill Gates, so that Microsoft would continue to produce Mac-compatible versions of its Office Software. This collaboration provided Jobs with the insight to develop a Windows-compatible version of iTunes. As we all know, this expanded the company's market in a colossal way. In the end, no one questions Steve Jobs' personal genius. Instead, insightful individuals simply recognize that an essential part of that genius has been his ability to reach out and engage valuable collaborators all along the way.

Other examples of people reaching outside themselves for inspiration include:

- Velcro was discovered by a man who was inspired while taking burrs off his dog.
- James Watt conceived the idea for the steam engine, the computer of its day, by watching a tea kettle boil.

Many innovators across the arts, sciences, business, sports, and myriad other fields have come to the same conclusion. They willingly acknowledge that inspiration and creative breakthroughs come from looking outside oneself.

I think it is in collaboration that the nature of art is revealed.

—Steve Lacy, jazz musician

From the earliest childhood on, I have had the strongest desire to understand and to comprehend whatever I observed.

—Charles Darwin

It's what you learn after you know it all that counts.
—John Wooden, UCLA basketball coach

With our new recognition of how important collaboration is in any creative endeavor, let's now begin to examine the role of several specific types of support that may help to promote creativity for individuals and groups, including: *proximity, criticism,* and *fieldwork.*

Proximity

Great discoveries and improvements invariably involved the cooperation of many minds.
—Alexander Graham Bell

Steve Jobs has been given much credit for the design of the Pixar Studios building. There were objections initially when he located the mailboxes and meal areas in the center of the building, far from some staff offices. However, he was very deliberate in this arrangement. He believed that by making it a necessity for developers of various types to walk past the offices of other creative teams on a regular basis, accidental collisions of mind and collision of ideas would occur. Attesting to the value of these chance collaborations, Ed Catmull remarked:

Our building, which is Steve Jobs' brainchild, is another way we try to get people from different departments to interact. Most buildings are designed for some functional purpose, but ours is structured to maximize inadvertent encounters. At its center is a large atrium, which contains the cafeteria, meeting rooms, bathrooms, and mailboxes. As a result, everyone has strong reasons to go there repeatedly during the course of the workday. It's hard to describe just how valuable the resulting chance encounters are.[7]

Pixar was not the first to reap the benefits of building design as a catalyst for creative collaboration. Bell Laboratories was a division of AT&T early on, when AT&T was the only phone company in the United States. This scientific research corporation was, in many ways, the Apple of its day, generating a multitude of inventions that have completely changed our world. For example, in 1947 they created the transistor that would later make computers possible and, several years later, their creation of a silicon solar cell led to the development of the solar powered devices we use today. The laser, fiber-optic cables, touch-tone telephones, fax machines, communication satellites, and the first computer programming languages were all introduced to the world by Bell Labs as well. The man given credit for creating this culture of creativity was Mervin Kelly. He, too, believed in the beneficial effects of proximity in creative development and designed the Bell building with very long hallways believing, correctly, that various people would run into one another by chance on their journeys down the corridors.

Before Bell Labs, in 1942, was Building 20 at the Massachusetts Institute of Technology—a scientific think tank. Scientists were housed in what was considered a "dreadful old building" with the task of creating new technologies, such as improved radar equipment that could assist with the war effort. As the lab expanded, new space was required, and Building 20 was all that could be found. Remarkably, within a handful of years, the teams in this less than ideal setting had achieved major breakthroughs in radar technology, which aided naval navigation and weather prediction, as well as in improving the Allies' ability to detect enemy submarines.

The scientists in Building 20 were undeniably brilliant. However, much credit for their achievements has been given to the odd, unpleasant nature of the building. The offices all faced a very long hallway—so long, in fact, that it was hard to see clearly from one end to the other. On treks down the corridor, scientists would invariably bump into other researchers. These accidental meetings were considered a critical contributor to the project's success. As author Jonah Lehrer writes: "Building 20 became a strange, chaotic domain, full of groups who had been thrown together by chance and who knew little about one another's work. Yet, by the time it was finally demolished in 1998, Building 20 had become a legend of innovation, widely regarded as one of the most creative spaces in the world."[8]

Creativity involves a large number of people from different disciplines working together to solve a great many problems. Creativity must be present at every level of every artistic and technical part of the organization.

—Ed Catmull, President, Pixar and
Disney Animation Studios

Preceding Apple, Bell, and even Building 20, we find Thomas Edison's lab, an extraordinary incubator of inventions and the creative team as well. As David Burkus describes in *The Myths of Creativity*:

The team at Menlo Park worked on various projects, some for Edison's clients, some for clients of their own, and even some side projects just for fun. They worked closely together, often sharing the same workshop space, despite being involved with separate projects. They shared machines, traded stories, and passed along insights or ideas they believed might be helpful for other projects or unknown future work. Their ideas and insights cross-pollinated. In some cases, they borrowed ideas and even physical parts from other projects.[9]

In more recent years, many organizations have continued to expand in new ways on the use of building design and proximity in purposeful efforts to maximize collaboration and incidental support opportunities between individuals and teams. For instance, one of the most successful airplane launches to date was the Boeing 777. Their chief executive at that time, Phillip Condit, helped to design the new building needed for the development and manufacturing processes. Like other successful leaders, Condit knew how important it would be for staff from different departments to intermingle and stimulate one another's creativity. In one attempt to maximize such interactions, he designed the new building with not only elevators, but escalators thinking that the slower ride to the next floors might provide greater opportunities for interaction and lead to chance conversations.

Google, too, benefits regularly form design features that enhance what they term ROC—"return on collisions." This organization is famous for its generous perks, including their gourmet meals. What many people aren't aware of, however, is that this benefit is designed to maximize employee creativity. Google tracks how long the cafeteria lines are, and they strive to keep the wait consistently at three to four minutes. This, they believe, will increase the likelihood that individuals will have time to visit with one another during the delay. Additionally, long tables are provided for employees to sit at during breaks and meals, improving chances that employees will sit across from or next to someone they don't know. As Geoff Colvin in *Fortune Magazine* writes: " . . . and it puts those tables a little too close together so you might hit someone when you push your chair out and thus meet someone new . . . the 'Google bump' as employees call it. And now we see the real reason Google offers all that fantastic free fare: to make sure workers will come to the cafeterias, where they'll start and strengthen personal relationships . . . the food is just a tool for reaching a goal, and the goal is strong, numerous, rewarding relationships."[10]

A study conducted by Ben Waber and colleagues clearly demonstrated this power of return on these social collisions. They studied the sales force of a large pharmaceutical company, tracking collaboration across occupations. The company wanted to increase collaboration across disciplines, so to accomplish this goal they decided to do something odd: they reduced the number of coffee machines. Previously, the company had provided one coffee machine for every six employees. They took out the smaller machines and built bigger ones, with an end result of one coffee maker for every 120 employees. They also created a larger, more attractive cafeteria, which became popular among staff. Individuals and teams from different departments began to bump into one another incidentally during coffee breaks and lunch time, and, within three months, sales had gone up 20 percent—*an extra 200 billion dollars.*[11]

If you are thinking that in this age of digital communication that these sorts of accidental collaborations or "collisions" are less critical than they were in less technologically advanced times, you would be wrong. Professor Thomas J. Allen of the Massachusetts Institute of Technology, who wrote the book *Managing the Flow of Technology*, was the first to identify what has come to be called "The Allen Curve."[12] This is a measure that associates how often employees communicate with one another with how physically close they are when they work. What Allen discovered was that employees were more likely to interact regularly with fellow team members who sat six feet or less away from them than those who were 60 feet away. This, of course, seems obvious. For many of us, however, this correlation may no longer appear to be relevant in today's world, because we can easily connect with others from anywhere at any time. As Waber put it: "It would seem that distance-shrinking technologies break the Allen curve and that communication no longer correlates to distance." However, when his team studied contemporary workplaces, they found that "both face-to-face and digital communications are still very relevant in the age of technology." In one study, engineers who shared a physical office were 20 percent more likely to stay in touch digitally than those who worked elsewhere. When they needed to collaborate closely, co-located workers e-mailed four times as frequently as colleagues in different locations, which led to 32 percent faster project completion times.[13]

In another interesting study of this type from Harvard Medical School, the effect of collaboration among researchers on the success of scientific papers was examined. Research success was defined by how many times a particular paper was cited as a reference in other research. The study examined a total of 35,000 papers, each written by two or more authors, and they matched the number of citations with the physical proximity of the co-authors. What they discovered was that the most successful research papers were written by authors who worked within 10 meters of one another.[14]

A great deal of current research, in fact, supports the essential nature of proximity in creativity and success. As a result, a relatively new phenomenon called "coworking spaces" has taken office collaboration to a new level during the past decade. In these spaces, individuals and groups share their working environment with others who are typically not employed by the same organization. They may work side-by-side with vendors, customers, and teams from other organizations to create products and services, or be inspired by observing others working in varied fields on projects quite different from their own.

Airbnb, for example, the thriving community marketplace where customers can rent a wide variety of unique accommodations, has a conference room in its San Francisco headquarters that anyone can rent and use to create such work groups. Zappos, the remarkably successful online retailer, also has a coworking space that is inhabited by their own employees, freelancers, neighbors living near the Zappos offices, and others. These more recently designed "hubs" appear to be the modern equivalent of Bell Labs and Building 20, providing networking opportunities and camaraderie, as well as what Rameet Chawla describes in *Entrepreneur* magazine as ". . . the intangible benefit of what I call *assisted serendipity*: a multitude of unexpected encounters that are difficult to recreate in traditional office settings and provide nearly immeasurable amounts of value for new businesses."[15]

Criticism

The question is, then, how do you develop an environment in which individuals can be creative?

> *I believe that you have to put a good deal of thought to your organizational structure in order to provide this environment.*
>
> —David Packard

While criticism and negative feedback can certainly make some people feel uncomfortable, current research maintains that a free flow of ideas along with healthy debate results in more quality solutions than the original model of brainstorming. This is true whether you are in the business world, education, the arts, or in any other creative setting. Team members who are set up to safely and effectively critique one another's ideas tend to experience more success.

David Kelly is founder of the design firm IDEO, one of the most innovative companies in the world. According to IDEO's general manager, brainstorming at IDEO is "practically a religion."[16] Employees are instructed to defer judgment and go for quantity. Although this sounds like a return to Osborne's strict rules on brainstorming, Kelly has expanded the original model and has developed a unique, clear set of rules for giving critical feedback as well. IDEO uses one of the cornerstone strategies of improvisational theatre called "yes and," in which people build upon others' ideas without negating them. In theatre, saying "yes" demonstrates acceptance of people's ideas as they are shared. Every new piece of information added helps to refine or redefine the idea as the concepts grow. In business, the process works that way as well. It is a way to begin the collaborative creative process on a positive note as discussion begins.

Pixar has an even more elaborate process for letting the director and team know when an idea they are proposing won't work. In a presentation at the Stanford Business School, Catmull began by stating that the first versions of movies often "suck." The line usually gets a laugh, but the message is quite important. Catmull's management genius is evident in his ability to create a safe structure in which creative teams can effectively discuss and address any noted "suckiness." The model that Pixar has developed is unique in the industry. It's based on the principle of developing creative teams where people can and must reach for support. Other studios purchase a script and then hire people to direct and act, but Pixar reversed this process and made hiring and managing people the first priority.

One manager leads each creative team. When Pixar's creative teams need help, they seek support from the "brain trust," a group consisting of John Lassiter and the eight senior directors who provide feedback (a.k.a. support). "This is all about making the movie better," says Catmull. "There's no ego. Nobody pulls any punches to be polite. This works because all the participants have come to trust and respect one another." The advising group has no authority, so a director is always free to take or leave the advice. Catmull believes that the lack of authority is crucial: "It liberates the trust members, so they can give their unvarnished, expert opinions and it liberates the director to seek help and fully consider the advice. It took us a while to learn this."

Everyone recognizes the challenges inherent in getting talented people to work effectively with one another. As Catmull describes it: "This takes trust and respect, which managers can't mandate; they must be earned over time. What we can do is construct an environment that nurtures trusting and respectful relationships and unleashes everyone's creativity. If we get that right, the result is a vibrant community where talented people are loyal to one another and their collective work . . . [And] everyone feels they are part of something extraordinary."[17]

Trust between people does not necessarily mean that
they like one another, it means that they understand one
another.

—Peter Drucker

Leaders in any meaningful endeavor have the responsibility for creating an environment where new ideas are welcome, even when—or possibly especially if—they contradict what leadership is already doing. The field of medicine for example, is constantly undergoing change for the betterment of the world. Creativity is at the core of this persistent metamorphosis at every level, from the development of the latest pharmaceuticals and robotic surgical techniques to the evolution of management and delivery of services in varied settings. One study, which sampled the effects of creativity in a medical setting, looked at quality improvement projects in intensive care units (ICUs) at 23 hospitals. What researchers found was that ". . . some units were identifying risks and coming up with ways to avoid future problems, while others were not because the people in them were terrified to speak up." They consistently noted that the units demonstrating the greatest quality improvement across time had managers who "asked questions, acknowledged their own fallibility or lack of knowledge, and appreciated others' contributions." In her summary, investigator Amy Edmondson highlighted the benefits of making things safe for people to share their concerns and ideas: "As a result, these units more quickly adopted new practices that reduced infection rates and led to other improvements in patient care."[18] The important point here is that, no matter what the field or endeavor might be, when leadership opens the door to construc-tive suggestions and creative input, the chances for individual and organizational success improve immeasurably.

> *Innovation usually emerges when diverse people*
> *collaborate to generate a wide-ranging portfolio of ideas,*
> *which they then refine and even evolve into new ideas*
> *through give-and-take and often heated debate. This*
> *collaboration should involve passionate disagreement.*
> *Often organizations try to discourage or minimize*
> *differences, but that only stifles the free flow of ideas and*
> *rich discussion that innovation needs.*
> —Linda Hill and Greg Brandeau,
> *Harvard Business Review*

Fieldwork

The most creative individuals and organizations put little stock in divine inspiration. Instead, they go out into the world and observe their customers to assess their needs and frustrations, then seek to create meaningful solutions. One of the most creative companies in the world today is the innovation consulting firm, IDEO. They helped Apple to develop the computer mouse, designed the first portable defibrillator, and created the first stand-up toothpaste tube! The company's strategy is to view themselves as anthro-pologists and to see their customers as a tribe to be observed and studied. This tactic appears to work exceptionally well, regardless of the organization type.

IDEO, for example, was hired by Kaiser Hospitals to try to improve the system used during shift changes. This is one of the most important and potentially dangerous times in a hospital, as vital information is passed from one group of nurses to the next. Omissions and misunderstandings during this critical transition time can result in harm to patients. IDEO stationed their team members at handoff points during shift changes to study what worked and didn't work. What they noticed was that the nurses spent 30 minutes at each shift change reviewing the patients' progress and planning for the next shift. The patients and families referred to the units as "ghost towns" for those 90 minutes each day. These were not times when they could reach for support when in need. Even worse, given fatigue and distractions, sometimes vital information was not shared or not heard. In response to these observations, IDEO came up with a simple, elegant solution. Instead of meeting with oncoming nurses as a group, each nurse going off shift would discuss the patient's situation and plan with the new nurse at the patient's bedside. The patient and family members then could listen, add information, and express their needs. In addition, a chalkboard was placed at the bedside for essential information about medications, procedures, etc., as well as listing the nurse on shift—the patient's primary contact for support. As a result of this fieldwork, errors were significantly reduced. In addition, nurses were more successful in their roles and patients were provided the support they needed to recover with greater ease.[19]

John Hopkins Medical Center identified a similar concern after a child died from a preventable medical error. In this case, fieldwork was undertaken by one of the center's physicians. While watching a European road race on television one night, he observed the extraordinary teamwork of the pit crew and wondered if their systems might be helpful in improving the hospital's systems. He went to Ferrari's racing team for ideas on improving shift change communication and the ideas he came away with worked![20]

As we reach the close of this chapter, let's return once again to Steve Jobs and Apple. It is useful for us to remember that this company has not invented any type of device. Instead, they have improved—usually dramatically—on existing products. The iPod, iTunes, iPad, iPhone, and everyone's new best friend Siri, were all built based on ideas or inventions originally created outside of the Apple corporation. The genius of Steve Jobs and the members of his team is in their fieldwork. They have been able to sustain their magnificent success in part by going out into the field to discover gems, along with their existing flaws, and have created solutions to make products better, easier to use, more stylish, or otherwise more compelling to their audience. They continually look for inspiration wherever they can find it.

Alex Portland, the Director of the MIT Human Dynamics Laboratory summarized how essential collaboration—reaching out—is to the creative success of any organization: "It is not simply the brightest who have the best ideas; it is those who are best at harvesting them from others. It is not only the most determined who drive change; it is those who most fully engage with like-minded people. And it is not wealth or prestige that best motivates people; it is respect and help from peers."[21]

The myth of the lone creator refuses to vanish. It is an attractive myth, the notion that one of us, if talented and inspired enough, can bring forth a work of art or breakthrough product. Individuals do invent remarkable things and create great beauty to be enjoyed by the world, but only with a little—or a great deal—of help from others. It is when people reach out and collaborate that creativity truly flourishes.

> *What a person thinks on his own without being*
> *stimulated by the thoughts and experiences of others is,*
> *even in the best of cases, rather paltry and monotonous.*
>   —Albert Einstein

CHAPTER 8

Relationships: Sustaining Intimacy and Trust

*If you want to go fast, go alone. If you want to go far,
go together.*

—African Proverb

The most famous little leaguer is a remarkable girl named Mo'ne Davis. She pitched in the Little League World Series—the first ever to pitch a no-hitter—and her athletic performance, poise, and humility earned her national media attention. Being 13, female, African-American, and from a low-income family added to her recognition. She was on the cover of *Sports Illustrated*, made the rounds on all the nighttime talk shows, and threw a perfect strike at a Dodger's game. This talented athlete became a role model for young girls throughout the country, due not only to her incredible skills on the field, but to her admirable character as well. A gifted child, you might say—and you would be right. But a closer look reveals a more complex story. Just where did those gifts come from?

There was a man, watching from the stands, when she pitched the no-hitter. He commented to Frank Bruni, editorial writer for the *New York Times*, that day: "What haunts me is that for every success we have, there are probably one hundred other kids who could be successes, but never had the opportunity. I hope this opened people's eyes. Kids given a chance will excel, whatever their economic background, whatever their race."[1] The man, Frank Bruni, was talking to Steve Bandura, Mo'ne's coach. Like all successful athletes of any age, race, or background, Mo'ne received the right kind of support when it was needed most. In her case, a big part of this came from Bandura. He had mentored her, helped her to believe in herself, and gave her the confidence and guidance to achieve extraordinary results.

Bandura did not do this just for Mo'ne, but for hundreds of children from the poorest neighborhoods of Philadelphia across decades. With no salary or funding, he established a little league for children ages five to eight, eventually expanding the age range and putting together a traveling team called the Monarchs. Mo'ne was one of those Monarchs. She and countless other children were recipients of Steve Bandura's gifts of support. Bandura taught his players about much more than baseball. He instructed them in manners and courtesy, teaching them how to effectively connect with others. He educated them in the history of the civil rights movement and, when his team was traveling, he took them to the Negro League Baseball Museum in Kansas City and to the graveside of Jackie Robinson and his players were required to write a report on Jackie Robinson and the story of All-Black Baseball. From this, they learned that role models can provide silent guidance and support when we are reaching for success as well.

I have scoured the Internet and could find almost no reference to Coach Bandura's amazing work, other than the beautiful article by Frank Bruni entitled "Black, White, and Baseball." It is not unusual, however, to find that those in the background, those who provide the backbone for success, are often spared the limelight. However, the recipient of his gifts is indeed a star. Mo'ne Davis became a powerful figure in the media, a success both on and off the field. Mo'ne was a role model with incredible athletic skills and a winning personality who also possessed the essential skills for success: she was willing to reach for support, accept help, and had the courage to allow this remarkable coach to nurture and guide her gifts. For any of us, it is this sort of attitude and the response of support that allows us to thrive in any area of life.

You may wonder why I have waited until now to address success in relationships, here near the end of our journey together. It is because, in the end, relationships are what every other chapter has been about. To address fear in the way we human beings are biologically designed to address it effectively, relationships are required. To reach for and receive the necessary support to achieve great things in any area of life—be it work, health, family, romance, even sports—relationships are required. Let's begin, then, to explore our relationships by tracing them back to their start, to our parents and earliest care providers—our first coaches.

Robert Frost once said, "Home is the place where, when you have to go there, they have to take you in." For some, home and family has always been a blessing, a place that you have been able to take for granted. In good times or bad, no matter what mistakes you've made or what tragedy card life may have dealt you, you knew that loving parents or family would be there for you. For others, this concept is an abstraction. You may feel that you are on your own, or that even if your parents are alive and well, they likely would not be your best choice for support.

Food, shelter, water, clothing—these "survival basics" are necessary in childhood, but they are not all that a child needs in order to thrive. The power of supportive relationships in reducing fear and quieting a child's alarm system has been demonstrated repeatedly in research. Consider, for example, the "Strange Situation Studies" developed by Mary Ainsworth.[2] In Ainsworth's original study, mothers and their 9- to 12-month-old infants were observed in natural interactions at home across several visits for a total of 72 hours prior to participating in a laboratory study. During each study episode in the lab, the mother was initially in the room with her child, along with another adult who was a stranger to the child. The mother was then instructed to leave the room while the stranger remained. When the mothers re-entered the room, some children rushed to them to be comforted and their distress from the separation quickly resolved. Ainsworth described these children as "securely attached." Other children hurried to their returning mothers, but they were hard to console, arching their backs away from their mothers, seemingly angry and frightened. These children she labeled "ambivalent-insecure." The third type of child appeared indifferent both when mother left the room and indifferent when she returned. This group she called "avoidant-insecure."

Most interesting to note when reviewing the findings was the very high correlation between the parenting styles observed at home during that first year and the children's subsequent behavior in the lab. Initially, some investigators argued that the avoidant children had simply learned to be more independent at a younger age, suggesting that this might actually be a desirable trait. However, later studies concluded that the avoidant children, although appearing indifferent at a surface level, had higher levels of the "stress" hormone cortisol in their bloodstreams. This suggests that they experienced more fear than those securely attached.

In a follow-up study, Dr. Mary Main exposed each of the three types of children to a scary situation (for example, mildly stressful events such as a live clown, a robot clown, and a puppet show). Their mothers were present, but they were asked not to provide comfort for the first three minutes. During the second three minutes, they were asked to comfort their children. The children who had been identified as securely attached, although appearing just as frightened as the ambivalent and avoidant groups, were the only ones who evidenced no increase in cortisol levels. In a similar study, cortisol levels were measured in 60 children about to get vaccinations. Once again, although all children reached for their parents in fear, the securely attached children were the only ones to have no increase in stress hormone levels. In both cases, as Dr. Megan Gunnar of the Institute of Child Development at the University of Minnesota described it: "The secure children seemed to be saying, 'This is scary but I feel safe.' They had the resources to cope."[3]

Research also demonstrates the importance of healthy relationships in childhood as a predictor of healthy relationships in adulthood. This can be clearly seen in the outcomes of the "Berkeley Longitudinal Study," in which Dr. Main selected infant-parent pairs from the Strange Situation studies and proceeded to follow them across the length of a generation. Each child once again experienced the Strange Situation scenario at age 6, and each of these 6-year-olds was given a Separation Anxiety Test (SAT) in which their response to pictures of children being separated from their parents was observed. Additionally, each parent participated in an Adult Attachment Interview (AAI). The correlations discovered were eye-opening. The 6-year-olds' responses to the Strange Situation correlated strongly with their responses as infants; the 6-year-olds' responses to the SAT produced the same results and percentages; and the parents responses on the AAI correlated highly with how their own children had behaved as infants. Most astounding, however, was the fact that when the infants reached age 19 and participated in an Adult Attachment Interview as well, the responses of these now young adults correlated precisely to their behavior in both of the Strange Situations scenarios and to their parents AAI responses! According to Main, "the Strange Situation predicts an infant's behavior for life . . . and the AAI proves it."[4]

What this suggests to us is that the type of response we tend to naturally lean toward in our relationships is often defined very early in our lives by the roles we have played with our primary supporters or, possibly, by the roles we have observed. If we are prone to develop secure attachments as children, that tendency will likely stick with us. If we are not prone to develop secure attachments, that tendency will likely stick with us as well— unless we do what is necessary to get it unstuck. In either case, it is essential that we eventually establish secure connections with the people who, as Dr. Main describes it, are our "havens of safety that must be approached in times of need." This is not only critical for the good health and proper development of a child, but it remains essential in adulthood. It underlies our ability to reach for support and, therefore, our success in all key areas of life.

Having the good fortune to be supported, nurtured, and mentored in childhood, then, is one of the most crucial needs we have. However, there are multiple ways in which a child's need for support may be thwarted, and it is easy for a child to go off course when parents are struggling. Some of the more common challenges I have encountered in my work include:

- Parents living through war, famine, financial crises, or other devastation who have little time or energy for the child;
- Parents who are struggling with a physical or psychological illness, or perhaps substance abuse, and lack the physical or emotional energy to nurture or respond to the child's needs;
- Parents who were minimally supported themselves as children, so they do not understand that responding to a crying or reaching child is crucial;

- Parents who are in physical pain or emotional distress who, due to a paucity of resources themselves, turn to the child for support (in these cases, the child takes on the role of parent, learning the skills of a giver while his or her own needs are suppressed);
- A parent dying when the child is young, leaving a surviving parent with limited time or skill in nurturing the child;
- Growing up in a family where another sibling consumes the parents' energy due to medical or other problems;
- Parents going through an angry divorce, which may leave little time or positive emotion for essential nurturing.

In many of these or similar situations, reaching out as a child may have seemed impractical, ineffective, or even dangerous. If you grew up in a family where going to your parents with your fears felt useless or scary, then as an adult it is typically much harder to recognize that you need and want support. It may still feel too dangerous, too risky—in any setting, with anyone in your life. However, children are not the only ones who require a safe, supportive environment in which to thrive. The process simply begins there.

To flourish, relationships of any kind, at any age or stage of life, depend on *intimacy* and *trust*. Intimacy is the ability to recognize and share your fears with another person. Trust is the confidence that sharing those fears will lead to support. Intimacy and trust are often difficult to achieve, however, because our greatest fear in any relationship is that if we open up and reach out to another person, we will be judged, criticized, abandoned, or betrayed. If we are to achieve success in our relationships, then, it is essential that we recognize and understand this natural fear at a deeper level.

Yet even although we may be greatly hurt again, we must risk it. I am boldly suggesting that the one essential element, the oxygen of *any* successful relationship—be it a romance, friendship, family, work, or any other connection—is our willingness to reach out and share our vulnerabilities and fears. Nothing is more critical in assuring that any relationship, in any setting, will succeed. And, nothing is scarier to us. So, just how do we get past this natural fear?

> Our greatest fear in relationships is that, if we reach out and open up to another person with our fears and needs, we may be judged, criticized, abandoned, or betrayed. And yet, the essential element, the oxygen of any successful relationship, is our willingness to reach out and share our vulnerabilities and fears.

Once again, an understanding of how the brain works may shed additional light on why this issue of fear and reaching for support is so vital to our success. Psychiatrist Stephen Karpman, originator of the Drama Triangle, believes he has discovered the biology of storytelling, as do I. This is based on two simple and profound observations. The first observation is the understanding that all cultures, all societies, have both stories and storytellers. No civilization has ever been found to be without them. The second observation is that all stories are created in the brain and heard, read, visualized, and processed by the brain as well. Anything that is so universal that occurs in a specific human organ must have a biology to it, right?

Karpman's Drama Triangle suggests that all stories have three basic elements: the *Persecutor* (the villain), the *Victim* (who often becomes the hero), and the *Rescuer* (who saves the victim). There is a simple childhood cartoon that provides a wonderful example of this, where the villain (the persecutor) ties up the beautiful damsel (the victim) and the hero (rescuer) comes to save her. Whether Black Bart, Dick Dastardly, or Snidely Whiplash comes to mind, this simple, recurring theme and cast of players demonstrates the key roles in any drama.

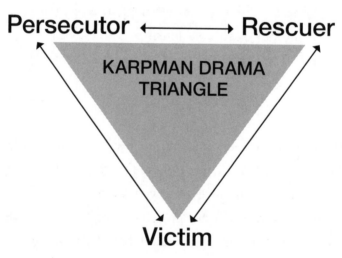

Image 8-1: The Karpman Drama Triangle.

In the original *Star Wars*, young Luke Skywalker (the victim) is minding his own business when along comes the Death Star (persecutor) to wipe out Luke's aunt and uncle. In response, Hans Solo and Luke (turned rescuer) go to rescue the Princess. These roles play out again and again in the stories we tell—and in the stories we live as well.

"So what does all of this have to do with biology?" you might ask, "And, more importantly, with me achieving success in my relationships?" Let's take a look at biology first. The Drama Triangle illustrates the essential survival mechanism in the brain. As hunter-gatherers tens of thousands of years ago, when we came across a stranger as we walked across the Savannah, our initial response would have been fear—amygdala activated. A good thing. Our first challenge would have been to ask ourselves, "Am I safe (or a potential victim)?" and "Is this person a threat (persecutor) or an ally (rescuer)?" A biologically driven drama triangle, act one. The handshake, in fact, is thought by many to have originated as a way to answer this biologically based question. We are "reaching out" to someone new with an empty weapon hand and observing their response. In a similar way, as we begin to develop a new friendship, romance, or a collaboration with colleagues we are, in effect, "emptying our hands of our defenses." When we greet an unfamiliar person, our first question even today is, "Is this person safe? Is he or she a potential ally, or someone dangerous?" The primary decision in any relationship, be it with a friend, romantic partner, colleague, or boss begins with the answer to this question: *"Am I safe?"*

The Drama Triangle is also quite useful in explaining why conflict between two people, especially romantic conflict, is frequently so hard to resolve. Consider this: when we have an argument with someone, which role are we fighting for sole possession of—persecutor, rescuer, or victim? The victim, of course! And what role are we trying to convince the offending party (not us, certainly) that they belong in? The persecutor, without a doubt. We want the other party to agree that they did something inconsiderate and hurtful, and we want them to change roles and rescue the situation by apologizing and making it up to us. Now that doesn't sound too difficult, does it? Not if you're the victim! The problem is, what position is the other party jockeying for? You've got it right—the same one. They want you to admit that you were wrong (persecutor), that you hurt them (the victim), and they want you to apologize for (rescue) the situation. With both people fighting for the victim position, solutions are generally impossible. It is possible to step outside of the Drama Triangle and look for solutions. However, it is far from easy.

Following is a brief exercise to help you begin to become more aware of how the Drama Triangle may play out in your own life:

Consider the following questions:

1. Do you tend to automatically fall into one of the three positions when a relationship is struggling? If so, which one? Did you have this role as a child?
2. When you are sharing the details of previous friendships, romances that have not worked out, or perhaps work or family relationships that persist with challenges, do you tend to tell the story from the persecutor, victim, or rescuer position, or do you step outside of the triangle and speak of lessons learned and the value gained from the other person?

What did you discover?

_____

The Drama Triangle can help us to better visualize this bio-logical connection between fear and support. The brain's amygdala and storyteller are constantly assessing: "Am I safe with this person or am I going to get hurt?" As we now know, when faced with a challenge the healthy brain wants us to reach for support. However, as we open up to another person and begin to share our perspectives, doubts, and mistakes, we worry about whether or not we will be respected, supported—rescued, so to speak. If not, then our greatest fear be realized. The person we reach out to may be a "persecutor" who will hurt or abandon us.

We define our best relationships as those people who know us well and accept us for who we are. These are the people in any setting or at any stage of life who stand by and support us when we reach out in times of need. And these are the people we wish to stand by and support as well. It is that relationship—two people standing outside of the triangle, reaching for and providing support—that leads to success.

> *Oh, the comfort—the inexpressible comfort of feeling safe*
> *with a person—having neither to weigh thoughts nor*
> *measure words, but pouring them all right out, just as*
> *they are, chaff and grain together; certain that a faithful*
> *hand will take and sift them, keep what is worth keeping,*
> *and then with the breath of kindness blow the rest away.*
> —Dinah Craik, *A Life for a Life*, 1859

So, what if we find it challenging—or even impossible—to develop or maintain these types of relationships in one or more settings? For example, perhaps you know someone who has shown up with his or her latest romantic interest and it takes you no more than about 20 minutes to figure out what it takes them 20 months, or perhaps 20 years, to discover—that they could not possibly achieve a sustained intimate relationship with this person? Or maybe you know a person who is persistently isolated at work, fighting for his or her own perspective, unable to make connections with colleagues, and pursing his or her projects alone. To understand why these things may happen, let's briefly revisit the three types of attachment.

Growing up without consistent support can make it very difficult to ask for or accept support from others as an adult. If your early attempts to reach for support were met with rejection or indifference, then you learned, when you're afraid, to pull up the drawbridge, fill the moat with water, and take care of things yourself. This may have been a brilliant decision when you were young. Learning to be self-reliant when there is no one to consistently rely on may have been a very good, perhaps even a lifesaving strategy. Unfortunately, the powerful decisions we make in childhood often become automatic patterns. As a result, habits of self-reliance frequently becomes justified rather than wise.

Do you recognize any similarity between the self-reliant, isolated adult and the response of the insecure-avoidant children in Ainsworth's Strange Situation studies? If there is a fear of being rejected or hurt that stems from your childhood or young adult experiences, then choosing a loving, caring, dependable friend or lover is too dangerous. It is too risky to wonder what it might mean if that type of person were to betray you. Even worse, we may have no awareness of our approach. Few adults, in fact, ever remember making the conscious choice to avoid asking for help. We don't recall when we decided to avoid becoming vulnerable or dependent, and our use of this strategy rarely gets revisited. As a result, by adolescence or adulthood, our choices of romantic partners, friends, and work alliances are often unfortunate. We may remain isolated and lonely or bounce from one poor choice to another, repeatedly experiencing abandonment, betrayal, or even significant harm (as in cases of abuse), with no awareness that the choices we are making are designed from within to avoid the vulnerabilities that were so painful in childhood.

Independence and self-reliance are essential skills at certain times in our lives. However if like competitiveness, these are only skills, it will detract from our ability to succeed in all of life's most important endeavors. Being free to choose to stand alone or to ask for help as needed in any given situation is true freedom and the key to our success.

So how do we go about developing strong, secure attachments if that is not our habit or our current habitat? It's true that children who received the support they needed from parents early on in life are blessed, as are adults who have forged and sustain relationships with supportive and nurturing people. However, as evidenced by Mo'ne's incredible athletic success under the wing of Coach Bandura, the meaningful support we all need can be provided by others along the way as well. The effects of good coaching, in fact, sound strikingly similar to the outcomes of those high-risk children in the Kauai Longitudinal Study who ended up thriving at ages 18 and 30 despite significant early life challenges. Recall that these children had the opportunity to establish a close bond with at least one person from whom they received nurturing during those first years of life—a relative, neighbor, baby sitter, or another caring adult who had stepped in to fulfill the nurturing role. Even in the heartbreaking tragedy of child abuse, we see examples of the power of support. It is a common myth that children who are physically or sexually abused by their parents will grow up to abuse their children. This is not consistently true. Children who are abused who have at least one nurturing and supportive parent, foster parent, or a kind and loving spouse in adulthood, report the least trauma at the time, the least damage as an adult, and they have a very low risk of repeating the abusive behavior.[5] What these findings tell us is that, regardless of circumstances, we all need nurturing people in our lives if we are to develop and sustain physical and mental health.

John McCarthy, like Bandura, organized baseball camps for a multitude of children in both Washington D.C. and in Brooklyn, New York through many years. He views baseball as a means of giving children the tools they need for a successful life. In a quote in *The Wall Street Journal* he remarked: "Good coaches are gardeners, and they grow human beings."[6] If you were choosing a coach to introduce you or your child to a new sport—or to anything important in life, for that matter—what would be your first priority? If you said, "Someone very skilled and accomplished at that thing," I'm afraid your answer would be wrong. Researcher Benjamin Bloom interviewed 18 tennis players who, at some point in their careers, had all been ranked in the "top 10 in the world." Bloom was looking for common traits to help explain their extraordinary accomplishments. One of the most consistent findings was that these players' first coaches were not necessarily prestigious in the sport, but they were all very accomplished, very skilled, in working with children, showing an interest in children, and helping children to fall in love with the sport. Bloom described these coaches as people who "liked children and rewarded them with praise, signs of approval, and even candy when they did anything right. They were extremely encouraging. They were enthusiastic about the talent field and what they had to teach these children. In many cases . . . they treated the child as a friend of the family."[7]

So perhaps it is time to identify and look for, and continue or begin to provide, such nurturing and support in our relationships now. Acknowledging our fear, reaching for and giving support, and strengthening our relationships throughout our lives all serve to decrease the feelings of "stress" that get in our way and to open the door to success in our work, health, and relationships. Whether we are talking about a romance or our connections with friends, family members, or colleagues, the quality of our relationships underlies our ability to reach out to others, which in turn underlies our potential for success in all key areas of life.

As we wrap up this chapter, let's take just a minute to recall one other long-term study mentioned in the Introduction. The Harvard Grant Study began in 1939 and has followed 268 male sophomores for 75 years. Researchers interviewed each of these students and their families extensively at the beginning of the project and each received medical exams and psychological testing to assess their health and well-being every two years. Astonishingly, 96 percent of the subjects who were interviewed were followed well into their 80s. The findings from the study were many, but they all boiled down to a single important point. A few years ago, George Vaillant, one of the most recent researchers in this lengthy project, was asked, "What have you learned from the Grant Study men?" His response? *"That the only thing that really matters in life are your relationships to other people."*[8]

CHAPTER 9

Why People Choose the Wrong Path . . .
And How to Re-Choose

*The mind is its own place, and in itself, can make a
Heaven of Hell, and Hell of Heaven.*

— John Milton, *Paradise Lost*

*The most valuable knowledge we can have is how to deal
with disappointment.*

— Albert Schweitzer

We all make choices. Some we make consciously, such as which
restaurant we might visit or which week we will vacation this

year. Others we make subconsciously, without really considering the options. This is often where choices based on fear are made. Mastering fear is about recognizing fear and calling it what it is— not stress, or anxiety, or worry, but fear. It is about becoming aware of our responses to fear and exploring our willingness to reach out for support. Achieving and sustaining the success we desire in all areas of life—in our work, our health, and our relationships— depends on these things. It is about *mastering the right reach* and helping others to do the same.

Perhaps you already have these skills well established and you are as successful as you care to be in all facets in your life. In this case, increasing your awareness as you have done may simply help you to help others succeed. Or perhaps, in reading this book, you have had an opportunity to recognize and re-examine your responses to fear in a new way. Possibly you have redefined stress and seen it from a new perspective, or maybe you've realized that your choice to reach out for support is not yet all you would like it to be. For those who have experienced this, you may now be in a position to begin to "re-choose." If you are one of the many disciplined, successful people who has experienced difficulty achieving and sustaining success in any area of your life, now may be time for you to reconsider the strategies that may have served you in the past but cannot help you to achieve the success you are seeking now or in the future.

So why do we choose not to reach? And, is it possible for us to make a different choice that will lead to greater success? To begin answering these questions, let me first share with you a story of a patient who was ready to "re-choose."

Daniel came to my office seeking help in ending a romantic relationship of seven years. He began our discussion by listing at length and in great detail the flaws he perceived in his partner. She was described as beautiful, but uneducated, and Daniel felt that she was not very organized or intelligent. He had ended this relationship multiple times, but somehow they always seemed to find one another again and resume. The woman was now interested in discussing the possibility of marriage and children, which added urgency to the visit. Daniel was seeking a strategy to end this on-again-off-again relationship once and for all.

The situation sounds somewhat simple, but a few additional questions revealed a much more complex dynamic. Daniel was uncomfortable being without a partner. Anticipating the close of his current relationship, he had already shared three dates with a new woman. She was highly educated, held a prominent position in a law firm, and was also very attractive. So, you might wonder, what was the problem? The new woman had two children and Daniel was certain he did not want to take on that responsibility. As I listened to Daniel speak about his current relationships and those in the past, a troubling pattern emerged. Daniel had a tendency to jump into relationships where the exit path was illuminated. He saw "deal breakers" from the beginning, which made it feel safe for him to reach out, although still painful to eventually exit.

So why didn't Daniel recognize his underlying fears? Why doesn't everyone choose the healthy response and reach for support? This powerful biological need of ours—to reach for support when we are afraid—is not an option. So why do we go off course and can we re-choose?

Culture and Competition

People go off course for three common reasons. The first is cultural. As you may recall from our earlier discussion, many Western cultures foster competition and individual effort as the number one path to success. American culture, in particular, places a premium on these skills. In many of our schools and jobs, success is based on the ability to out-smart, out-connect, or somehow out-perform the kid or colleague sitting next to us. Our personal stories, and the stories told around us, often reflect this in the tenacity and perseverance of the cowboy or detective or comic book hero overcoming great struggles. Our Olympic champions, famous actors and actresses, and business wizards like Warren Buffet also give the impression that talent and hard work are the recipe for success as well. As we've mentioned before, there is nothing inherently wrong with individual competition. It is not wrong to embrace the values of individual autonomy, freedom, and opportunity. These have served each of us well in specific endeavors in life, and being very good at this skill is one of the reasons you are successful today.

For those who wish to achieve and sustain success, however, we must also develop this same level of skill in our collaboration with others. This can be challenging. If you are part of a friendship, a romance, a family, or if you work with other people—pretty much if you do anything but exist all by yourself—reaching out and collaborating with others is what allows us to flourish. Most of life is a team sport. So we must be of two minds, embracing competition and collaboration simultaneously or selectively as is required in any given situation. We have a great tradition of working together to achieve excellence that we can use as a basis. American history, and the histories of many of our icons and idols, have been selectively written to reflect our focus on individual grit and achievement. When we learn of the Revolutionary War, we are typically not told of how much support our fledging country sought and received to make the war a success. However, we couldn't have done it without support. The French provided ships and advisors. The Dutch loaned us money to help finance the war. We have not succeeded in any endeavor alone. And, whether it is well-publicized or not, our individual icons know they had support as well. Olympic champions know the value of an excellent coach; Warren Buffett gives credit for his acumen to his mentor; actors acknowledge their acting coaches who taught them this very challenging craft.

Some of us have been blessed with family, outside supporters, or role models early in our lives, or perhaps partners, friends, or colleagues in our adult lives who have helped to embed this lesson and cultivate the skills of collaboration. Others now have the opportunity to do so. As you begin now to explore your choices, both past and future, the primary question for you to consider is: *"Am I as free to collaborate as I am to compete—and am I as accomplished in this skill as I would like to be?"*

Relationship Experiences

There is a second reason, much closer to home, as to why we may go off course in learning to reach for and accept support. This has to do with our family lives while growing up, and we've discussed portions of this in the previous chapter. If you were a child who went to your parents with a nightmare and one of them responded with, "Shut up and go back to sleep or I'll give you something to cry about!" then you learned early in life to avoid asking for help at all costs. Although this parent may sound cruel, sometimes the intention is pure. Parents are always preparing us for the world they grew up in. If your parent lived through immigration, world wars, and financial or relationship hardships, they may believe it essential to "toughen you up" to be sure that you can survive and endure in a world like the one they experienced.

The problem is the world is always changing and what was intended to be helpful may have been harmful. If your parent(s) frequently yelled or sent you back to bed alone, then you may have learned to be self-reliant as a strategy for living safely. Asking for help was too painful, too dangerous. Unfortunately, our decision to avoid asking for help at all costs is rarely revisited in adulthood. As a result, people may find themselves choosing romantic partners, business associates, and friends who don't have the skills to commit or comfort. We may choose people who could not possibly reciprocate or, if they did, it might make us uncomfortable. It is a painful way to live. Consciously, we want everything that a good relationship can offer, but unconsciously we may choose all the wrong people to invest in.

Another way we might go off course related to our early family experiences is much more subtle. Imagine that there is a time machine waiting outside your door to take you back in time into your childhood. You have the choice of entering either your mother or father's body and living out their marital existence as husband or wife. Which body would you choose? If you answered "neither" or "can I have a third choice?" it may reflect your confusion in childhood and the discomfort you felt when one parent dominated another. Stereotypically, mom may have been warm and caring to us during the day, but when dad came home, he was dominating or perhaps even bullying. In these cases, mom may have seemed to shrink, unhappy with the arrangement. Or, these roles may have been reversed. The important point is, if you grew up observing an imbalance, there is a good chance that you said to yourself, "When I grow up, I will never let that happen to me." Typically, that decision doesn't stay with us consciously, but instead becomes another automatic pattern: "I will never become dependent on anyone."

You may pride yourself on your independence and self-reliance, but when these skills are based on a fear of trusting others and resistance to asking for help, it frequently leads us to choose unreliable, undependable people for our mates and friends, and we may end up viewing other employees primarily as competitors rather than colleagues. This, too, can be a very painful way to live. Consciously, the rational brain wants a loving, caring partner, friends who are loyal and generous, and colleagues who are collaborative and appreciate. But the emotional brain, established in childhood, is more intent upon never getting hurt like the dependent parent was than in choosing the right people to invest in.

Consider this story to illustrate how this pain in childhood results in adult relationship problems:

When I first moved to Los Angeles many years ago, I became friends with a woman who, with much excitement, bought herself a brand new Porsche. This Porsche was the fulfillment of one of her bucket-list items and was a very big deal for her. We took this beautiful car to the grocery store and walked out with our food only to discover that the car had been stolen! My friend's upset was short-lived, since the insurance company promptly replaced the car. Two weeks later, she returned to the grocery store (a different one, of course) and, after making her purchases, she walked out once again to an empty parking space. Two brand new cars stolen in one month's time! My friend then went out and bought a used Chrysler and, from that point forward, her trips to the store became uneventful.

Now this may seem to have been a reasonable solution to her transportation needs and an understandable response to her fears of going to the store with no means of getting home and, possibly more importantly, of owning something that others might take away. However, metaphorically speaking, some people make this same decision about relationships throughout their adult lives. They have been hurt, abandoned, or betrayed too many times in childhood or in their young adult lives, and they can't bear the pain of any more rejections. So, they may choose friends, lovers, colleagues, and even employers who are not likely to provide the love, comfort, or support they need. They choose people they can never get close to and, therefore, protect themselves from ever being hurt again as painfully as they were hurt in earlier years. If a violent husband, a friend who gossips, or a boss who is relentlessly critical goes away, they will be relieved. If they risk loving someone truly able to reciprocate, however, the fear of being hurt again can be overwhelming.

Do you recall from our earlier discussions any other family patterns that may create a habit of avoiding support as well? One is having a parent or spouse who is out of control with his or her anger and/or alcohol or drug use. If it was never safe to rely on that person, you may have made yourself a promise to never end up like him or her. If you promised yourself that you would never lose control, then allowing yourself to experience emotions and become vulnerable to another person by expressing these is much too dangerous. Alternately, if you came home from school regularly to a parent who needed you to parent them (perhaps due to depression, emotional pain, physical illness, or social isolation), you may have become their support instead of the other way around. Children who grow up with the identity of a giver often forget their need for support or they believe that others aren't capable of providing it, and they find that asking for anything in their adult life is unfamiliar and uncomfortable.

Tabernacle Choir

There is nothing either good or bad, but thinking makes it so.

—William Shakespeare, *Hamlet*

In addition to a competitive culture and our early relationship experiences, there is a third reason we haven't yet explored as to why people may go off course in acknowledging fear and reaching for support. This is perhaps the most subtle and most powerful reason. Many of us have a built-in, critical voice that attacks us, punishes us, and reminds us of all of our current flaws and past sins each time the amygdala is activated. Alhough many of us have this critical voice, we are often unaware of it because it lives in our subconscious and has been there all of our lives. We think it is us.

Let me illustrate this for you in the same way I would for an audience. I ask those sitting in front of me, "How many of you believe that rejection is painful?" Virtually everyone raises their hand, staring at me, wondering why I would ask such a foolish question. I then say, "Let me try to prove to you that this is not possible!" The audience is usually intrigued at that point, although suspicious. "Now rejection can come in many forms, but romantic rejection is one type, correct?" Heads nod in agreement. "And romantic rejection has many forms. But I suspect you would agree that this is one type." I walk up to a woman in the audience then and ask her name. I say to her, and to the group, "If I approach this woman and say, 'Sally, would you like to go out with me Saturday night?' and Sally responds by saying, 'I'd love to but I'm flossing,' would you consider that rejection? Would it be painful?" The audience laughs and agrees that this is one form of rejection and that would be painful.

I then say, "Let me show you that this is not the case. If I asked Sally out and she gave me that lame excuse, as I walked away from her, which of two voices would I most likely hear inside my head: Door Number One: "Boy, Bob am I proud of you! That was gutsy! Could have been a little smoother . . . next time it'll be better . . . but I'm so proud of you for trying!" Through all that time, the Mormon Tabernacle Choir, 300 voices in my head, is singing the Hallelujah Chorus form Handel's Messiah because I am living at risk and pursuing my dreams. Or, Door Number Two: I walk away hearing this voice shouting inside my skull, "No wonder she doesn't want to go out with you! You are such a loser! You're old, you're ugly, you're fat . . . nobody likes you . . . and nobody ever will!" I turn to the audience then and pose the important question: "Which response is more likely?" They respond, recognizing their own personal version of Door Number Two. After a pause, I gently ask, "So where was the pain? In Sally saying 'no' or in the conversation in my head afterward?"

To illustrate how this harsh, critical voice is connected to fear—to the amygdala—I then ask, "Does that voice show up at the best of times or the worst of times?" Universally, the audience responds, "The worst of times." As long as the amygdala is quiet, I tell them, our cortex is usually pretty good at making good decisions. But when the amygdala is activated by a doctor scaring us with a diagnosis, a relationship that is floundering, a work reversal, a child or friend in need, etc., the harsh voice shows up. It pounds on us when we are most vulnerable and, because we are not often aware of it, it tends to win the fight.

A new patient, Debbie, came into my office clearly frustrated. She was my first patient of the afternoon and she had come directly to my office from lunch. Her voice tone and words revealed frustration with herself. "Why am I always overeating?" she asked. "I didn't need to finish the whole sandwich or that piece of cake. What's wrong with me?" I remarked on the fact that she appeared angry with herself and she was skeptical when I suggested that the anger may be causing or at least contributing to her dietary challenges. I asked her if she would describe herself as critical. She replied, "Never of other people . . . but I'm hard on myself." I asked her for an example of this that wasn't related to food. She said, "I'm learning to play golf and I'm mad at myself every time I hit a bad shot." She added, with a wry grin, "Which is most of the time."

After a quiet moment she volunteered, "I've never thought about it before, but I come from a military family and there were lots of rules. Dinnertime was never fun. I ate fast so I could leave the table quickly." Another pause. "I never realized how hard I am on myself." I suggested that she felt pressure all day to be productive and disciplined, and that perhaps food was the only consistent relief she got from the pressure. I explained how food also calms the amygdala for the moments we are eating. As she was painfully aware, as soon as she stopped eating, the harsh voice inside returned to beat up on her food and portion choices, and many other aspects of her life as well. Her amygdala—her fear—was activated once again and she had no Tabernacle Choir response.

Whether the challenges are connected to our work, health, or relationships, many of us experience this harsh voice as a first response. It is activated by fear and, when we hear it, we need to reach for support—outside of ourselves or within. Near the end of this chapter, I've provided an exercise to help you begin this process of "reprogramming" the harsh inner voice. Your biggest challenge will be recognizing and accepting what I hope Sally's dating rejection demonstrated: *We are never responding to a situation, but to the conversation in our head about it.* This is a crucial aspect of changing our inner voice.

To help you understand this a bit more, take a moment right now to recall a person who has been very hurtful to you at some time in your life. Imagine sharing with me all the examples of their inconsiderate behavior or cruelty. After you finish relating your examples, imagine that I hold up their MRI, PET, or CAT scan and convince you the reason this person has behaved so poorly is due not to failures on their part or yours, but rather a slow growing inoperable brain tumor pressing on the frontal lobe, the part of the brain responsible for making good judgements and anticipating consequences of actions. Would this change your attitude and response? For most people, the answer is yes. But what has changed? This person's unkind behavior didn't change. The only change is the story in our heads about *why* they did what they did.

A second powerful example of the effect of the harsh inner voice can be found in a story told by Stephen Covey.[1] He describes a time when he was riding the New York subway and a man came into the car and sat down with his three children. As the train began its journey, the man's children chased one another up and down the car, unchecked and misbehaving, their childish shrieks adding to the loud, unpleasant noises of the old train. Covey's head was full of judgment for these spoiled children and their irresponsible parent. As the situation grew from bad to worse, Covey's inner conversation grew in its harshness. After a while, the father came by to sit down beside Covey and blurted out, "Please forgive my children. We just came from the hospital. Their mother just died." Do you think this changed his attitude toward this family? In a heartbeat! Our biggest challenge when we hear the harsh inner voice (about ourselves or others) is to recognize and remember that we have the potential—a strong potential—to change our emotional responses to circumstances.

It is hard to overstate the damage that this harsh voice can do, especially when we are not aware that it's speaking. As we begin to reach to others for support and experience the healing effects of this, we want to be especially aware of the messages we are giving ourselves and the power that these messages have to control or free us. The harsh voice increases our fears. It is very difficult to ask for or accept help if the harsh voice is telling us that we are weak, or that the other person will judge us or think us incompetent for asking. It is hard to feel safe and loved in a friendship or romance if the harsh voice inside is telling us that we are unlovable. It is hard to enjoy a promotion or the challenge of a job if the harsh voice says we are impostors about to be exposed. And it is hard to accept and enjoy a compliment if the only voice you trust is the harsh one you hear in your own mind. In short, the harsh voice is one way of explaining how frequently the disorders of anxiety and depression occur. These are complex disorders, but one way of understanding them is to recognize that when fear is greeted by the harsh voice, it becomes anxiety; and when sadness is responded to by the harsh voice, it becomes depression. If a nurturing voice soothes our fears, anxiety and depression might never appear.

The good news is that, if you become aware of the harsh voice, you can learn to see it as a relic of childhood that has outlived its usefulness. If you recognize it as something that needs to be reprogrammed to be more constructive, to work for rather than against you, then you are two-thirds of the way home. If we can change this harsh inner voice into a more caring and creative version, it will calm the amygdala, giving us back our cortex and the ability to creatively problem solve. This is not, however, always easy to do. If it were, we'd find that our species would be more peaceful and kind to one another.

Working to silence and reframe our harsh voice reduces its power. Sometimes, however, the noise remains until the reprogramming is complete. To help you begin the process of reprogramming, let's take a look at some harsh messages that clients have shared with me and some of the alternative messages they were able to come up with. Then, you may want to try coming up with a few of your own.

Harsh Messages	Alternative Messages
I am a failure.	I made a mistake. What can I learn from this?
I'm worthless.	I am being too hard on myself. I can correct whatever I have done wrong.
I shouldn't be in pain. I'm weak.	This is a crisis for me. It's natural to hurt. It's a sign of strength to live with pain and grow.
Don't ask others for help. They will think less of me.	Asking for help is a good thing. I can't control what others think.
I'm too old to be making these mistakes.	Life is a series of lessons. I am here to learn and grow.

What examples of "harsh messages" can you come up with from your own life? What might be good alternative messages for these?

For some people, the harsh inner voice is occasional and mild. For others, or at specific times in life, it can be persistent and extreme. A true anxiety disorder can be crippling and individuals with persistent anxiety may fight desperately to rid themselves of the intense discomfort. A simple explanation for anxiety is "a fear of being afraid." A common presentation of anxiety is that, first, a person begins to feel symptoms of fear, such as a racing heartbeat and shortness of breath. The harsh inner voice says, "Nothing is right, everything is wrong." The cortex does not provide any comforting words or reassurance, but instead throws gasoline on the fire, by saying to the amygdala, "You're having a heart attack, you're dying." As a result, symptoms escalate. The sensations are terrifying and the anxious person often looks for any solution, from prescription (or nonprescription) medication to avoiding any and all situations believed to trigger the anxiety and panic. A technique called cognitive behavioral therapy, somewhat similar to the reprogramming of the harsh inner voice described previously has proven effective for many individuals with this disorder.

In cases of less persistent anxiety, the research on the positive effects of reprogramming the harsh voice is especially remarkable. At Duke University, 40 freshmen who were struggling academically were selected to participate in a study. They were riddled with self-doubt and were at high risk of dropping out of school. The students were divided into two groups. The control group, unfortunately, were left to their own devices to cope, whereas those in the experimental group were provided several levels of support. They were given information about how common it was for college students to struggle during their first year and they were provided mentorship support via a film, in which upper classmen shared their struggles during their first years of college and provided reassuring statements that things would get better with time. The freshmen who viewed the films then wrote an essay about how their personal experiences compared to the stories and perspectives shared on the video. In this way, the intervention provided not only direct support to the students in the form of information and coaching, but it also provided a possible "inner" script—content for reprogramming the freshmen's harsh inner voice. The results were dramatic. The students who had viewed the films and written the essay ended up with grade point averages that were much higher than those who did not receive this help, and these students were also more likely to seek mentors and tutors to help them to achieve these excellent results.[2]

One of the most powerful tools for transforming fear is to write a short essay on one's values and how those values are lived out during day-to-day activities. Writing this specific essay for 10 minutes is enough to empower and strengthen the inner voice in response to fear. In repeat studies, this activity has been correlated with better physical health, improved school performance, and increased effectiveness at work. If you were only going to do one exercise to strengthen your inner voice—what we are calling your "Tabernacle Choir"—this would be the one you'd want to select. However, fortunately, there many other additional options as described in the following.

Steps for Reprogramming the Inner Voice and Creating a Tabernacle Choir

1. Your first step is to identify the harsh voice. Assume every time you are upset, the harsh voice is present. I recommend strongly that you stay with this step until every time you are upset, you automatically look for the voice. That will lay a strong foundation for the rest of the steps.

2. Whenever possible, write down what the harsh voice has to say so that you begin to separate you from the harsh voice.

3. Once you have mastered an awareness of the harsh inner voice, it becomes possible to change the voice to a more Tabernacle Choir version. To do this, select one of your written examples of the harsh voice and write down what a nurturing and supportive voice would say in the same situation. This can be challenging. Your goal is to make the words inspirational. If you are having trouble writing this nurturing voice, try to imagine what you might say to a child or best friend if he or she were in the same situation.

4. Practice using this technique several times a day if possible, whenever the harsh voice arises. You'll often recognize it when your amygdala is activated—when you feel anxious, stressed, and worried—in other words, whenever you are afraid.

5. Speak the words aloud, in a nurturing tone of voice, one to two times each day. This, too, will help in reprogramming. The harsh voice will be overwritten with the nurturing one.

Now that you've started the process of reprogramming your mind's automatic response, the ultimate challenge will be for you to be patient with yourself. The harsh voice will likely try to join the party, saying things like: "Hurry up! Why isn't this working for me already? I told you what a loser you are!" Expect this. Change is hard for everyone—even your subconscious. If you are hearing the harsh voice in response to your nurturing attempts, your goal is to be aware of it and hear it as a backlash response to your reprogramming efforts rather than a valid message. Once again, at that moment, gently reconstruct the kind, loving, patient voice you would use with others you care for deeply and practice replacing the harsh voice both in that moment and again later that day. Remember, your brain will learn this new skill better with patience and practice.

As you continue reprogramming, your awareness of fear will grow. This is a good thing! The following suggestions are provided to help you to further your skills in becoming more aware of fear and responding in the one healthy way that leads to success in all areas of life.

Steps for Learning to Reach for Support

1. If you need reminders that reaching for support is part of the hero's journey and that it is crucial for success, consider doing one of the following:

   a. Read *Opening Up* by James Pennebaker.[3] It will remind you of the many benefits of reaching for support in all areas of life and will provide you with some additional, practical, and valuable tools as you begin to increase your reach.

   b. Re-read the quotes throughout this book that deal specifically with reaching for and providing support. Select and post those that are especially meaningful to you and review these regularly.

   c. Read the biography of a person you greatly admire and see if you can identify all the people who helped them along their path.

2. Begin to explore where your reluctance to reach for support may have started. If you believe that it started in childhood, consider these questions:

   a. Did your parents have difficult childhoods and was it simply that they could not teach you what they never learned?

   b. Were your parents struggling with their own battles (emotional, relationships, financial, etc.) and they simply found the task of attending to a child too overwhelming?

    c. Was one of your parents quite needy and so came to you for support or were they unable to care for children and you were placed in a role of caring for your younger siblings?

3. As you were encouraged to do in an earlier chapter, imagine what a loving friend or parent might provide you if you were to choose to reach for support. Repeat this process daily if possible:

    a. Imagine a best friend, a kind boss or colleague, a tender lover, or even a Yoda or Fairy God Mother. Once or twice a day, ask yourself: "If I could have exactly what I want from this person at this moment in time, what would it be?"

    b. Be kind to yourself if the response to this question is silence. It may take a little while for the brain and heart to reopen this channel to your desires.

    c. The wants don't have to be practical or reasonable; children's wants can be unrealistic. You are not yet trying to receive specific support, but instead to recapture the childhood longing for support.

4. Next, begin reprogramming your brain to learn to reach for support with people in your daily life. Start by asking yourself this question two or three times a day: "What type of support would I like from the person in front of me at this moment in time?" If your childhood and/or adulthood has been challenging, you are likely to hear silence for a while until your brain gets the hint that you are serious. With enough gentle

repetitions of the question, the channel to your longings and needs will reopen and you will start to hear your wishes for support. Be gentle with yourself and your partner or friends, since some of your desires may be irrational or unreasonable given the limitations of the person in front of you, but that is fine. You don't have to say them out loud.

5. You want to train your brain to reach toward people, rather than turn away from people in times of need. To do this, you can use a technique called "mind sculpture" to rehearse this new behavior. If you are interested in learning more specifics for this technique, see the discussion in Ian Robertson's book *Mind Sculpture*[4] or in my book, *One Small Step Can Change Your Life.*[5] A brief description of the process to get you started is:

   a. Picture an ideal friend or lover in front of you. Look into their eyes as you picture yourself sharing your fears and confessions with them.

   b. Picture them responding in an ideal, loving way to your revelations.

   c. Repeat this imagery exercise once or twice a day for a few seconds each time.

6. Take an inventory of the people in your life. Do you have family, friends, an employer, colleagues, and others in your life who are caring and nonjudgmental?

   a. If the answer is yes, then the next question is, have you asked them for what you need or have you been hiding your needs from them or resisting when they offer help?

b. If you have chosen people who are not generous, you can choose to keep them in your life. However, out of fairness, don't expect them to change as your awareness of your needs increases. You may need to let go of some of them, or perhaps add new people to your life who show up interested in reciprocity, capable of and wanting to give.

Steps for Helping Others Learn to Reach for Support

1. The biggest challenge in helping others to learn to reach for support is convincing the person they need to seek something they have never experienced. My friends who ski or skydive love these activities and they seek out opportunities to participate in them frequently, often at great expense. I have never skied downhill or skydived, and I'm told I have no idea what I am missing. I've no desire to find out, either! This may be the response others have if you suggest you want them to become aware of their fears and learn to reach for support. You will need to be patient as you try to convince others that they need to risk being vulnerable. There are two questions I often use to plant the seeds that you too may want to try:

a. If you had a young daughter or son who was scared, would you want them to keep their fears to themselves or bring their distress to you?

b. If I as your friend (or colleague or lover) was struggling, would you want me to keep things to myself or be honest with you and seek your guidance and support?

   No one has ever given me a wrong answer to these questions. They simply have started to create doubts about rationalizations for avoiding the fears of leaning on others.

2. If they are interested in reading, give them the book *Opening Up*, by James Pennebaker, or perhaps the book you are reading now.

3. Ask them if they ever went to their parents for support as a child, maybe when they had a nightmare, faced a bully or harsh teacher at school, or experienced some other childhood challenge involving fear. If the answer is no, explore this in greater depth if they will allow you to. Ask gentle questions to help them become more aware. Possible questions might include:

a. Were there any teachers or friends you chose to confide in?

b. Do you think your parents could go to their parents for help?

c. What happened when you went to your parents for help? What happens when you go to other family members now?

d. Do you choose to confide in your friends, work associates, life partner, etc., at this time in your life?

4. Ask them about their friendships, work relationships, and romantic partners in the past. Have they chosen people who are reliable and dependable, who insist on giving as well as taking? Would they like to do so now?

5. Be a role model. Share your own vulnerabilities and mistakes with humor and compassion. This is essential!

6. You may choose to offer them the opportunity to lean on you, or you may decide to offer them some small examples of support without making it formal. Examples might include:

   a. Offer to treat them to coffee or a meal.
   b. Send them a card or e-mail with words of praise just to let them know you were thinking about them.
   c. Share a confidence with them to role model the behavior you are encouraging.
   d. Invite them to share in an activity.
   e. Brag about them to another person in front of them or to someone who might relate the compliment to them.

7. If opening up to you or to someone else is too big of a step, ask them if they would be interested in journaling about their feelings for 15 minutes or less each day. More is not necessary. I often encourage people to burn or flush the pages, for two reasons. The first is that people are sometimes afraid to put honest

emotions on paper for fear that someone in the house will find and read them. The second reason is that in writing, you are trying to *release* the feelings, not store them for the future.

8. Ask them what their fears (or concerns) would be if they did open up to a friend, family member, colleague, or to a lover.

9. Suggest that they create a "job description" for the ideal friend or lover. Encourage them to be highly specific.

10. Reassure them that fears show up in the best of relationships and that the fears will come and go, but people can gain strength in their relationships by having the opportunity to reassure one another.

11. Be patient as you coach and mentor. It's possible that they may have avoided support in order to survive. With the right input, the brain can change this. However, if their brain erroneously believes that avoiding being vulnerable to others is what still allows them to survive and flourish, the change does not come quickly.

12. Be aware of your own beliefs about the person you are supporting. Numerous studies have demonstrated that your expectations for others have dramatic, positive effects. Your expectations also influence your willingness to invest time and energy and your commitment to respond warmly and empathically. Believe that your support will make a change.

Obstacles to Collaboration in Organizations

Many businesses *preach* cooperation, collaboration, and team work. However, *achieving* an environment with a robust habit of asking for and giving support often poses a significant challenge. This is primarily because organizations verbally encourage collaboration, but reward competition. Businesses tend to reward the top salesperson, the top-performing manager, or the most creative problem-solver with praise and bonuses, while others who contribute to the successes look on with envy or anger. Dr. Heidi Gardener, faculty member of the Law and Business School at Harvard, has summarized this dilemma elegantly:

> . . . it's no secret that the organizational structure, compensation systems, and culture in many, if not most professional services firms, favor individual contributors rather than team players. Up-or-out promotion systems encourage rivalry among junior associates and the competitive values become so ingrained that the winners find it counterintuitive to collaborate when they become partners . . . Few professionals truly work alone, but coordinating with peers across departments is significantly harder than delegating to junior staffers in your own department whose skills are similar (but inferior) to your own, and whose advancement depends on pleasing you.[6]

Leonard Sayles has researched managers' styles across two decades. He cynically provides the following summary of "promotional tips" for managers in unhealthy organizations: "Avoid confrontation, withhold suggestions for improvement, do not ask your boss to champion 'unpopular' positions, always agree with your boss, concentrate on presentation skills, and always look good in meetings with superiors."[7] If these are the rules for success in your organization, whether you are a manager or employee, you may want to consider "re-choosing" as soon as possible.

Reaching for support in business, as we mentioned before, is most critical when an employee first finds a mistake or thinks that maybe something isn't going the way it should. Do employees in your organization feel safe bringing their doubts, fears, and concerns to supervisors? Too often in business today, the answer is no. There is nobody saying, "Bring us your worries." There is no organizational "Tabernacle Choir" asking, "What can we do to solve this? What can we learn from this? And how can we thank you?" And, more often than not, constructive criticism is erroneously confused with "negativity," and it is not welcome. As a result, small mistakes are ignored until they become too large to overlook. The tragic Deepwater Horizon oil spill in the Gulf of Mexico, the largest accidental marine oil spill in the history of the petroleum industry, provides a distressing although common example of this sort of approach. There were more than 200 small spills on that platform before that fateful night, but it was hard to get the attention of the supervisors or the oil company. A series of cost-cutting decisions, shortcuts, insufficient safety systems and, probably most importantly, decisions to repeatedly overlook the alarms raised by employees and collaborating organizations were blamed for the catastrophe.

A powerful example of how an organization might change a culture too afraid to ask for help is demonstrated in the work of Alan Mulally at Ford Motor Company. Mulally, who had overseen the construction of the Boeing 777, transitioned to Ford in 2006 after being denied the CEO job at Boeing. Ford was a mess at the time, with $30 billion in overall losses and poor prospects for the future. Very early in his tenure, Mulally gathered a roomful of marketing, engineering, and manufacturing managers from Ford Divisions throughout the world. The assembled staff had created 260 files, each representing one aspect of the assembly process for each of Ford's models. Mulally gave each manager three cards— one red, one green, and one yellow. The green was to indicate that they were experiencing no problems; the yellow card meant the factory was experiencing minor issues; and the red card indicated significant manufacturing problems. Mulally asked these executives to attach a card to each file, green, yellow, or red. Mulally was stunned to find that there were no red or yellow cards at all, given Ford's $17 billion in losses that year alone. As kindly as he could, he asked, "Team, is there anything not going well?" His question was met with silence and eye contact went to the floor.

The following week, Mulally asked the same question once again. This time, Mark Fields, head of Ford Canada, held up a bright red card. He was responsible for the launch of a new model, the Ford Edge, and there was a serious problem with the tail gate. Fields had stopped production and was admitting a serious mistake. Mulally described the moment when the bright red card appeared in the following way: "The room got silent. What is this new guy going to do now? He said it was gonna be safe . . .

He said he wanted to know what the situation was . . . I started to clap."[8] Just to be sure that the others got the message, he added: "Mark, this is great visibility!" After 12 seconds, someone in the room suggested a solution; and 12 seconds after that, someone else offered to help. The next week the card was yellow, and the next week it was green. Mulally's message was now clear to the entire Ford team: mistakes were to be admitted, concerns noted, and help was going to be available. By the next week, the entire stack of 260 files looked like a rainbow.

Organizational Steps: Reaching for Support

1. To assess your organization's health, begin by asking the following questions:
   a. Are staff penalized or rewarded for asking for help?
   b. Do team members feel safe to report their doubts, concerns, and mistakes?
   If the answer to this is "yes," how is this communicated to staff?

2. Are you a manager or team member who regularly models acknowledging fear and asking for help (reaching for support)?

3. Are the "givers" in your organization able to set limits so they can support others and still fulfill their responsibilities? What can be done to assist those who need help in this area?

4. How is conflict expressed and resolved in your organization? For example:

   a. Are there rules for how people are expected to give critical feedback?

   b. Are there clear rules for resolving disagreements?

   c. If you are a manager, have you made it safe for staff to criticize you?

   d. If you have made it safe for staff to bring fears, problems, and mistakes to you, how have you achieved this?

5. As a manager or team member, how do you encourage disagreement or divergent points of view in a team?

6. Consider the following suggestions for running a meeting:

   a. Begin by letting the team know what the process is going to be. Will decisions be made with a "majority rules" approach or does the leader or manager make decisions after receiving input from the team?

   b. Inform the team regarding the issue at hand and let them know that you've started to brainstorm solutions (use the plural!). Then, ask each member to contribute his or her ideas.

   c. If possible, set up small pilot projects so that teams can discover for themselves how various solutions might or might not work.

7. Like Gordon Bethune of Continental Airlines, who turned around a struggling organization with small

rewards for all employees based on the group's on-time performance, or Robert Iger, CEO of Disney, who compensates his staff based on the performance of the whole company rather than each division, contemplate making financial rewards contingent on group success rather than individual accomplishments. This gives every individual an incentive to collaborate, to confront problems, and to share information—because achieving things individually isn't going to make a payment on the next car.

8. Assure that every individual team member is informed, at the outset, what their specific role is in the organization and what information and expertise they are expected to provide.

9. If you are part of an organization that is not yet "healthy," you might consider asking yourself, "Am I modeling the behaviors that I would like to see this organization bring into play and am I demonstrating the values I would like the organization to live by?" If you have people reporting to you, is your team a model that is likely to inspire others due to the team's performance and the way they interact with one another and throughout the organization?

The human tendency is to wish for, or expect, others to change first. However, as Gandhi once said, "Be the change you wish to see in the world."

CHAPTER 10

The One Essential Skill

We don't accomplish anything in this world alone . . . and
whatever happens is the result of the whole tapestry of
one's life and all the weavings of individual threads from
one to another that creates something.
—Sandra Day O'Connor, Supreme Court Justice

We are meant to reach to another for support. This is the natural, optimal human response to fear and it is the one essential skill for achieving and sustaining success in our work, health, and relationships. If you grew up in a loving, supportive family or community, or if you are now part of one, you are very fortunate. You may be able to take for granted the security that this provides. It may confuse you, however, when people turn away or become hostile in response to your efforts to comfort or help them. If, on the other hand, you grew up or live now without the gift of support, odds are high that you have not consistently sought out the connections and help you need to quiet the amygdala and achieve the peace you need to secure or sustain the success you desire in one or more areas of life.

Although you may have wisely walled off this need to reach out early in life, you may no longer have an awareness of how critically important it is for each of us to acknowledge our fears and seek solace or support in most of life's endeavors. You may have become fiercely independent and competitive and, although you may believe that these skills are what allowed you to succeed in the world (which may be true), perhaps they have also limited or crippled your ability to create supportive friendships, to participate effectively on teams at work, or to develop the loving, intimate relationship you desire. The toll on your body for denying this need may have already begun to appear.

The good news is that at any time, you can re-choose. With the awareness and skills you have developed as we have journeyed together, you can add to your competitive savvy the skills of collaboration, closeness, comfort, and care. There are two key challenges that have been presented to you in this regard. The first is for you to become more aware of your many fears—both conscious and subconscious—and then learn, or re-learn, how to reach out to others for the help and support you need. To be successful in this, you must see this reaching out as a strength rather than a weakness. The second, larger challenge is for you to begin building the support you need from within. To be successful in this, you will need to develop your own nurturing inner voice—what we have called your "Tabernacle Choir Voice." This voice can calm the amygdala and free you from fear, just as a loving, caring parent or partner might do. This nurturing voice will allow you to admit that you are afraid and will invite you to reach out and seek whatever help you may need.

The best definition of optimism I have ever seen is: *Optimism is what you say to yourself when life is not going well.* And, no matter how things have been going for you until now, I am optimistic that you will succeed.

As I wrote these pages for you, my purpose was three-fold. I wanted to:

- Help you become more aware of fear, and recognize it as a powerful ally;
- Encourage you to reach for support, which is the optimal response to fear; and
- Share with you tools and strategies that will help you to nurture yourself and others toward success in all key areas of life.

Success is going from failure to failure without loss of enthusiasm.

—Winston Churchill

Never confuse a single defeat with a final defeat.

—F. Scott Fitzgerald

It is what people say to themselves when they fail, and whether or not they are willing to reach for the right kinds of support, that determines their ultimate success. Many successful people before us have faced challenges and adversity along their way. R.H. Macy failed seven times before his store succeeded. Dr. Seuss' first children's book was rejected by 23 publishers, William Faulkner's first novel by 18, and *Harry Potter* by 12. Oprah Winfrey was fired from her first job as a reporter, Walt Disney was fired from a newspaper job because he "lacked imagination," and Michael Jordan was dismissed from his high school basketball team for lack of talent. Obviously, none of them gave up. As Michael Jordan puts it: "I've failed over and over and over again in my life and that is why I succeed." Those who succeed learn to nurture themselves and they make sure that there are others surrounding them who can encourage them during the long dark days when they are striving—then celebrate with them when they succeed.

I didn't see it then, but it turned out that getting fired from Apple was the best thing that could have happened to me. The heaviness of being successful was replaced by the lightness of being a beginner again, less sure about everything. It freed me to enter one of the most creative periods in my life.

—Steve Jobs

CHAPTER NOTES

Introduction

1. William McNeill, *Plagues and Peoples* (New York: Anchor Press, 1976).
2. Emmy Werner and Ruth Smith, *Overcoming the Odds: High Risk Children from Birth to Adulthood* (Ithaca: Cornell University Press, 1992).
3. Joel Shurkin, *Terman's Kids: The Groundbreaking Study of How the Gifted Grow Up* (New York: Little, Brown & Co, 1992).
4. George Vaillant, *Triumphs of Experience: The Men of the Harvard Grant Study* (Cambridge: Harvard University Press, 2012).
5. Sheldon Gleuck and Eleanor Gleuck, *Unraveling Juvenile Delinquency* (Cambridge: Harvard University Press, 1950).

Chapter 1

1. Kelly McGonigal, *The Upside of Stress* (New York: Penguin, 2015).
2. Ed Catmull, *Creativity, Inc.* (New York: Random House, 2014).
3. Ed Catmull, "How Pixar Fosters Collective Creativity," *Harvard Business Review*, September 2008, 66.
4. Susan Jeffers, *Feel the Fear and Do It Anyway* (New York: Ballantine, 1998).
5. Yu, Gao, Raine, Adrian, et al. "Association of Poor Childhood Fear Conditioning and Adult Crime," *American Journal of Psychiatry*, 167, 1 (2010): 56–60.
6. Kelly McGonigal, *The Upside of Stress* (New York: Penguin, 2015).

Chapter 2

1. Redford Williams, *Anger Kills* (New York: Harper Collins, 1998).
2. Roger Fisher and William Ury, *Getting to Yes: Negotiating Agreement Without Giving In* (New York: Penguin Books, 2011).

3. Jochim Hansen, Susanne Winzeler, and Sascha Topolinski, "When the death makes you smoke," *Journal of Experimental Social Psychology*, 46, 1 (2010): 226–228.

Chapter 3

1. Emmy Werner, "Resilience and Recovery: Findings from the Kauai Longitudinal Study," *Research, Policy, and Practice in Children's Mental Health*, 19, 1 (2005): 11–14.
2. Herbert Spencer, *Principles of Biology*, 1864. Out of print. Details of the use of the term "survival of the fittest" can be found in any reference to the work of Herbert Spencer.
3. Isaac Newton, *The Correspondence of Isaac Newton* (Massachusetts: Cambridge University Press, 2008).
4. Henry Ford, *My Life and Work* (New York: Create Space, 2013).
5. Jeff Bezos interview on *The Charlie Rose Show*, June 27, 2001.
6. Howard Schultz, "What's Brewing at Starbucks," *Business Week*, March 31, 2011.
7. Shelley Taylor, *The Tending Instinct* (New York: Times Books, 2002).
8. Beth Azar, "A New Stress Paradigm for Women," *Monitor on Psychology*, 31, 7 (2000): 42.
9. Muzafer Sherif, "Superordinate Goals in the Reduction of Intergroup Conflict," *American Journal of Sociology*, 64, 4 (1958): 349–356.

Chapter 4

1. Henri Nouwen, *Out of Solitude: Three Meditations on the Christian Life* (Notre Dame: Ave Maria Press, 2004).
2. Joan Borysenko, *Guilt is the Teacher, Love is the Lesson* (New York: Hay House, 2008), 178.
3. Denzel Washington, "The Mentors He'll Never Forget," *Guidepost Magazine*, January 2013, 4.

4. Carol Dweck, *Mindset: The New Psychology of Success* (New York: Random House, 2006).

5. Po Bronson, "How Not to Talk to Your Kids," *New York Magazine*, August 3, 2007: 34.

6. John Gottman, *Why Marriages Succeed and Fail* (New York: Simon & Schuster, 1994).

7. Jim Collins, *Good to Great* (New York: Harper Business, 2001), 75.

8. www.shsxc.com/quotes.aspx.

9. John Mackey, interview in *The Harvard Business Review*, January 2011, 122.

10. David Owen, "Betting on Broadway," *The New Yorker*, 1994, 60, 17, 60–73.

11. Martin Seligman, *Learned Optimism* (New York: Vintage, 2006), 32–33.

12. Sally Kline, *George Lucas Interviews* (Mississippi: University Press of Mississippi, 1999).

13. www.alberteinsteinsite.com.

14. L. Winnerman, "Restaurants Serve Social Sustenance," *Monitor on Psychology*, 37, 9 (2006): 20.

15. Kevin Johnson, "Stockton School Massacre: A Tragically Familiar Pattern," *USA Today*, April 2, 2010.

16. Associated Press, "Five Children Killed as Gunman Attacks a California School," *New York Times*, January 18, 1989.

17. Doris Kearns Goodwin, *Team of Rivals: The Political Genius of Abraham Lincoln* (New York: Simon & Schuster, 2005).

18. John Wooden, http://thisibelieve.org/essay/i-am-better-than-i -used-to-be/. Accessed October 16, 2015.

Chapter 5

1. Christopher Cardoso, "Oxytocin and Emotional Oversensitivity," YouTube, www.youtube.com/watch?v=CIaarjIuVls, January 14, 2014.

2. Daniel Goleman, "Thriving Despite Hardship: Key Childhood Traits Identified," *New York Times*, October 13 1997: D1.

3. Meyer Friedman and Ray Rosenman, *Type A Behavior and Your Heart* (New York: Random House, 1985), 63.

4. Redford Williams, *Anger Kills* (New York: HarperCollins, 1998).

5. J.A. Kulik and H. Mahler, "Social support and recovery from surgery," *Health Psychology*, 1989, 8, 221–238.

6. R. Sosa, et al., "The Effect of a Supportive Companion on Perinatal Problems, Length of Labor and Mother-Infant Interactions," *New England Journal of Medicine*, 303 (1980): 11–14.

7. Marshall Klaus and Jon Kennell, "Effects of Social Support During Parturition on Maternal and Infant Mortality," *British Medical Journal*, 293 (1986): 585–587.

8. "Couples May Be More Likely to Get Healthier Together," *Monitor on Psychology*, 46, 4 (2015): 30.

9. L.G. Russek and G.E. Schwartz, "Perceptions of Parental Caring Predict Health Status in Mid-Life: A 35-Year Follow-Up of the Harvard Mastery of Stress Study," *Psychosomatic Medicine*, 59, 2 (1997): 144–149.

10. C.B. Thomas and K.R. Duszynski, "Closeness to Parents and the Family Constellation in a Prospective Study of Five Disease States: Suicide, Mental Illness, Malignant Tumor, Hypertension, and Heart Disease," *Johns Hopkins Medical Journal*, 134, 5 (1974): 251–259.

Chapter 6

1. Judith Valente, "United Crew Credits Training for Helping to Save Plane During Crisis," *Wall Street Journal*, March 3, 1989.

2. Pat Riley, *The Winner Within* (San Francisco: Berkeley Press, 1994).

3. David Burkus, *The Myths of Creativity: The Truth About How Innovative Companies and People Generate Great Ideas.* (New York: Jossey-Bass, 2013).

4. R. Suri, "Improving Affordability Through Innovation in the Surgical Treatment of Mitral Valve Disease," *Mayo Clinic Proceedings*, 88 (2013): 1075–1084.

5. Robert Huckman and Gary Pisano, "The Firm Specificity of Individual Performance: Evidence from Cardiac Surgery," *Management Science*, 52 (2006), 473–488.

6. Boris Groysberg, Linda Lee, and Asish Nanda, "Can They Take It With Them? The Portability of Star Knowledge Workers' Performance," *Journal of Organizational Behavior*, 29 (2008): 1213–1230.

7. Tom Junod, "How John Lassiter Raised the Children of America," *Esquire*, May 30, 2011, 30–36.

8. Ed Catmull, "How Pixar Fosters Collective Creativity," *Harvard Business Review*, September 2008, 65–72.

9. Fredrick Reichheld, "Lead for Loyalty," *Harvard Business Review*, July-August 2001, 76–84.

10. Daniel Coyle, *The Talent Code* (New York: Bantam, 2009), 64.

11. Adam Grant, *Give and Take* (New York: Viking, 2013).

12. Ibid.

13. David Rowan, "For LinkedIn Founder Reid Hoffman, Relationships Rule the World," *Wired*, March 20, 2012, 20–24.

14. Francis Flynn, "How Much Should I Give and How Often? The Effects of Generosity and Frequency of Favor Exchange on Social Status and Productivity," *Academy of Management Journal*, 46 (2003): 539–553.

15. Geoff Colvin, "Why Do Some Companies Keep Attracting and Holding Onto the World's Best Talent?" *Fortune*, March 15, 2015, 107–110.

16. Martin Nowak, "Why We Help," *Scientific American*, 2012, 307, 1, 35–39.

17. Salvatore Maddi, *Hardiness: Turning Stressful Circumstances Into Resilient Growth* (New York: Springer, 2012).

18. Karl Weick, *Managing the Unexpected* (New York: Wiley, 2007), 13.

19. Amy Edmondson, "Learning From Mistakes is Easier Said Than Done: Group and Organizational Influences on the Detection and Correction of Human Error," *Journal of Applied Behavioral Science*, 32 (1996): 5–28.

20. Jeffrey Liker, *The Toyota Way* (New York: McGraw-Hill, 2004).

21. Sara Mosle, "Building Better Teachers," *The Atlantic Monthly*, 2014, 314, 2, 42–44.

22. Ira Glass, "561: NUMMI," *This American Life on NPR Radio*, July 17, 2015.
23. Thomas H. Klier, "How Lean Manufacturing Changes the Way We Understand the Manufacturing Sector," *Economic Perspectives*, 17, 3 (1993): 2–10.
24. John O'Neil, "Vital Signs: Stress—Gauging the Boss Factor," *New York Times*, April 22, 2003.
25. Ed Catmull, *Creativity, Inc.* (New York: Random House, 2014).
26. Jonah Lehrer, "Groupthink: The Brainstorming Myth," *The New Yorker*, January 30 2012.
27. Joe Labianca, Hongseak Oh, and Myung-Ho Chung, "The Ties That Bind," *Harvard Business Review*, October 2004, 36.
28. Adam Grant, *Give and Take* (New York: Penguin, 2013), 151.
29. Keith Ferrazzi, "Candor, Criticism, and Teamwork," *Harvard Business Review*, January 14, 2012.
30. Howard Schultz, "I Could Smell Things Were Wrong," *Business Week*, April 4, 2011, 102.

Chapter 7

1. John Briggs, *Fire in the Crucible: The Alchemy of Creative Genius* (New York: St. Martin's Press, 1988).
2. "Artistic Influences: Paul Gauguin," Van Gogh Gallery, www.vangoghgallery.com/influences.
3. Colin Duriez, *Tolkien and C.S. Lewis: The Gift of Friendship* (New York: Paulist Press, 2003).
4. Neal Gabler, *Walt Disney: The Triumph of the American Imagination* (New York: Vintage, 2007).
5. Walter Isaacson, "The Real Leadership of Steve Jobs," *Harvard Business Review*, April 2012, 46–52.
6. Gary Wolf, "Steve Jobs: The Next Insanely Great Thing," *Wired Magazine*, www.wired.com/wired/archive/4.02/jobs_pr.html.
7. Ed Catmull, "How Pixar Fosters Collective Creativity," *Harvard Business Review*, September 2008, 71.
8. Jonah Lehrer, "Group Think: The Brainstorming Myth," *The New Yorker*, January 2012, 22–27.

9. David Burkus, *The Myths of Creativity* (New York: Jossey-Bass, 2013), 108.

10. Geoff Colvin, "Why Do Some Companies Keep Attracting and Holding On to the World's Best Talent?" *Fortune*, March 15, 2015, 107–110.

11. Ben Waber, Jennifer Magnolfi, and Lindsay Greg, "Workspaces That Move People," *Harvard Business Review*, October 2014, 69–77.

12. Thomas J. Allen, *Managing the Flow of Technology* (Cambridge: MIT Press, 1977).

13. Ben Waber, *People Analytics* (New York: Financial Times Press, 2013).

14. Jonah Lehrer, "The Brainstorming Myth," *The New Yorker*, January 2012, 22–27.

15. Rameet Chawla, "What's the Benefit of Co-Working Spaces?" *Entrepreneur*, www.entrepreneur.com/article/230446.

16. Jonah Lehrer, "Groupthink: The Brainstorming Myth," *The New Yorker*, January 30, 2012.

17. Ed Catmull, "How Pixar Fosters Collective Creativity," *Harvard Business Review*, September 2009, 65–72.

18. Amy Edmondson, "The Competitive Imperative of Learning," *Harvard Business Review*, 86, July/August 2008, 60–63.

19. Tom Kelley, *The Art of Innovation* (New York: Crown Business, 2001).

20. "The Checklist: If Something So Simple Can Transform Intensive Care, What Else Can It Do?" *The New Yorker*, December 10, 2007.

21. Geoff Colvin, "How to build the perfect workplace," *Fortune*, Fortune.com/2015/03/05/perfect-workplace.

Chapter 8

1. Frank Bruni, "Black, White, and Baseball," *The New York Times*, August 23, 2014.

2. Mary Ainsworth, *Patterns of Attachment: A Psychological Study of the Strange Situation* (New York: Psychology Press, 2015).

3. Beth Azar, "The Bond Between Mother and Child," *APA Monitor*, September 1995.

4. Karen Robert, "Becoming Attached," *The Atlantic Monthly*, February 1990, 47–70.

5. Joan Kaufman and Edward Zigler, "Do Abused Children Become Abusive Parents?" *American Journal of Orthopsychiatry,* 57, 2 (1987): 186–192.
6. Laura Meckler, "A Mom-Centered Approach to Sports," *The Wall Street Journal,* May 2, 2015: C3.
7. Daniel Coyle, *The Talent Code* (New York: Bantam, 2009), 176. See also: Benjamin Bloom, *Developing Talent in Young People* (New York: Ballantine Books, 1985) for more detailed discussion of the initial coaches of successful performers.
8. Joshua Wolf Shenk, "What Makes Us Happy?" *The Atlantic,* www.theatlantic.com/magazine/archive/2009/06/what-makes -us-happy/307439/.

Chapter 9

1. Stephen Covey, *Principle-Centered Leadership* (New York: Fireside Press, 1992).
2. Kelly McGonigal, *The Upside of Stress* (New York: Avery, 2015).
3. James Pennebaker, *Opening Up: The Healing Power of Expressing Emotions* (New York: Guilford Press, 1997).
4. Ian Robertson, *Mind Sculpture* (New York: Fromm International, 2000).
5. Robert Maurer, *One Small Step Can Change Your Life* (New York: Workman, 2014).
6. Heidi Gardner, "When Senior Managers Won't Collaborate," *Harvard Business Review,* March 2015, 75–82.
7. Leonard Sayles, "The Importance and Evolution of Leadership," Slideplayer.com/slide/2693230. See Slide #73.
8. Alan Mulally, interview on PBS, *The Charlie Rose Show,* July 27, 2011, www.youtube.com/watch?=0Y3z-9YC96Y.

REFERENCES

Ainsworth, Mary, and Mary Bleher. *Patterns of Attachment.* Washington, D.C.: Psychology Press, 2015.

Allen, Thomas J. *Managing the Flow of Technology.* New York: Taylor & Francis, 2006.

Angier, Natalie. "In helpless baby, the roots of our social glue." *The New York Times,* March 3, 2009, D4.

Azar, Beth. "The bond between mother and child." *American Psychological Association Monitor,* September 1995, 28, 4.

Bachelder, Kate. "How to save American colleges." *Wall Street Journal,* 25 (2015): A9.

Berkun, S. *The Myths of Innovation.* Sebastopol, CA: O'Reilly Media, 2007.

Bloom, Benjamin. *Developing Talent in Young People.* New York: Ballantine Books, 1985.

Borysenko, Joan. *Guilt is the Teacher, Love is the Lesson.* New York: Hay House, 2008.

Briggs, John. *Fire in the Crucible: The Alchemy of Creative Genius.* New York: St. Martin's Press, 1988.

Bruhn, John, and Stewart Wolf. *The Roseto Story.* Norman: University of Oklahoma Press, 1979.

Bruni, Frank. "Black, white, and baseball." *The New York Times,* August 24, 2014, 3.

Bryant, Adam. "Good C.E.O.'s Are Insecure (And Know It)." *The New York Times,* October 10, 2010, B2.

———. *Quick and Nimble.* New York: St. Martin's Griffin, 2014.

Burkus, David. *The Myths of Creativity.* New York: Jossey-Bass, 2014.

Burrows, Peter. "Welcome to Apple world." *Business Week,* July 9, 2007, 89–92.

Businessweek. "The best performers." March 26, 2007, 59.

Catmull, Ed. "How Pixar Fosters Collective Creativity." *Harvard Business Review,* September 2008 65–72.

————. *Creativity, Inc.* New York: Random House, 2014.

Collin, Jim. *Good to Great.* New York: Harper Business, 2004.

Colvin, Geoff. "Why Do Some Companies Keep Attracting and Holding Onto the World's Best Talent?" *Fortune,* March 15, 2015, 107–110.

Coyle, Daniel. *The Talent Code.* New York: Bantam Books, 2009.

Cruwys, Tegan, Alexander Haslam, and Genevieve Dingle. "The new group therapy." *Scientific American Mind,* 2014, 25, 5, 61–63.

Darwin, Charles. *On the Origin of Species by Means of Natural Selection, or the Preservation of Favored Races in the Struggle for Life.* November, 1859.

Doherty, William, Helmut Schrott, et al. "Effects of spouse support and health beliefs on medication adherence." *The Journal of Family Practice,* 1983, 17(5), 837–841.

The Economist. "A market for ideas." 2009, 392 (8649), 75–76.

————. "Lessons from Apple." 2007, 383 (8532), 11.

————. "Return of the stopwatch." January 23, 1993, 69.

————. "The Rise of the Creative Consumer." 2005, 374 (8417), 59–60.

Edmondson, Amy. "Learning from mistakes is easier said than done: Group and organizational influences on the detection and correction of human error." *Journal of Applied Behavioral Science,* 1996, 32, 5–28.

————. "The competitive imperative of learning." *Harvard Business Review,* July 2008, 60–63.

Ferrazzi, Keith. "Candor, criticism, and teamwork." *Harvard Business Review,* January 2012, 14.

Fisher, Roger, and William Ury. *Getting to Yes.* New York: Penguin, 2011.

Flynn, Francis. "How much should I give and how often? The effects of generosity and frequency of favor exchange on social status and productivity." *Academy of Management Journal,* 2003, 46, 539–553.

Fortune. "The greatest entrepreneurs of our time." 2012, 165, 5, 74.

Friedman, Howard, and Leslie Martin. *The Longevity Project.* New York: Penguin, 2011.

Friedman, Meyer, and Ray Rosenman. *Type A Behavior and Your Heart*. New York: Random House, 1985.

Gardner, Heidi. "When senior managers won't collaborate." *Harvard Business Review*, March 2015, 75–82.

Gilbert, Susan. "Benefits of assistant for childbirth go far beyond the birthing room." *The New York Times*, May 19, 1998, 23.

Gleuck, Sheldon, and Eleanor Gleuck. *Delinquents and Non-Delinquents in Perspective*. Cambridge: Harvard University Press, 2013.

Goleman, Daniel. "Thriving despite hardship: Key Childhood traits identified." *New York Times*, October 13, 1997, D1.

———. *Emotional Intelligence*. New York: Talent Smart, 2009.

Goodwin, Doris Kearns. *Team of Rivals*. New York: Simon & Schuster, 2006.

Gottman, John. *Why Marriages Succeed and Fail*. New York: Simon & Shuster, 1994.

Grant, Adam. *Give and Take*. New York: Viking, 2013.

Groysberg, Boris, Linda Lee, and Ashish Nanda. "Can they take it with them? The portability of star knowledge workers performance." *Journal of Organizational Behavior*, 2008, 29, 1213–1230.

Halberstam, David. "How he got up there." *Time*, June 22, 1998, 62–63.

Hansen, Jochim, Susanne Winzeler, and Sascha Topolinski. "When the death makes you smoke." *Journal of Experimental Social Psychology*, 2010, 46, 1, 226–228.

Huckman, Robert, and Gary Pisano. "The Firm Specificity of Individual Performance: Evidence from Cardiac Surgery." *Management Science*, 2006, 52, 473–488.

Hyatt, Josh. "Engineering inspiration." *Time Magazine*, 2010, 175(22), 44.

Jeffers, Susan. *Feel the Fear and Do It Anyway*. New York: Random House, 2006.

Jetten, Jolanda, Alexander Haslam, and Catherine Haslam. *The Social Cure: Identity, Health, and Well Being*. New York: Psychology Press, 2013.

Kaiser, Robert, Robert Hogan, and Bartholomew Craig. "Leadership and the fate of organizations." *American Psychologist*, 2008, 63, 96–110.

Kaufman, Joan, and Edward Zigler. "Do abused children become abusive parents?" *America Journal of Orthopsychiatry*, (April 1987), 186–192.

Keller, Abiola, Lauren Litzelman, et al. "Does the perception that stress effects health matter? The association with health and mortality." *Health Psychology*, 2014, 31, 5, 677–84.

Kivimaki, M., et al. "Justice at work and reduced risk of coronary heart disease among employees." *Archives of Internal Medicine*, 2005, 165, 2245–2451.

Klaus, Marshall, John Kennel, et al. "Effects of Social Support During Parturition on Maternal and Infant Mortality." *British Medical Journal*, 1986, 293, 585–587.

Krumholz, H.M., et al. "The prognostic importance of emotional support for elderly patients hospitalized with heart failure." *Circulation*, 1988, 97, 958–964.

Labianca, Joe, Hongseak Oh, and Myung-Ho Chung. "The Ties That Bind." *Harvard Business Review* (October 2004), 36.

Labianca, Joe. "The Ties That Blind." *Harvard Business Review*, October 19, 2004, 43.

Lamb, Kevin. "Strong social relationships important to good health." *The Arizona Daily Star*, December 19, 1999, 1.

Lehrer, Jonah. "Groupthink: The Brainstorming Myth." *The New Yorker*, January 30, 2012, 22–27.

Leslie, Connie. "Will Johnny get A's?" *Newsweek*, July 8, 1996, 72.

Liker, Jeffrey. *The Toyota Way*. New York: McGraw-Hill, 2004.

Maddi, Salvatore, and Suzanne Kobasa. *The Hardy Executive: Health Under Stress*. Chicago: Dorsey Professional Books, 1984.

Marshall, J.R., and D.P. Funch. "Social environment and breast cancer: A cohort analysis of patient survival." *Cancer*, 1983, 52, 8, 1546–1550.

Maurer, Robert. *One Small Step Can Change Your Life*. New York: Workman, 2004.

McGonigal, Kelly. *The Upside of Stress*. New York: Avery, 2015.

McNeill, William. *Plagues and Peoples.* New York: Anchor Press, 1987.

Monitor on Psychology. "Couples may be more likely to get healthy together." 2015, 46, 4, 30.

Mosle, Sara. "Building better teachers." *The Atlantic Monthly,* 2014, 314 (2) 42–44.

The New York Times. "Gauging the boss factor." April 22, 2003, D5.

———. "What innovation takes." February 26, 2012, 1, 6–7.

Nowak, Martin. "Why we help." *Scientific American,* 2012, 3–7(1) 35–39.

Ornish, Dean. *Love and Survival: The Scientific Basis for the Healing Power of Intimacy.* New York: Harper, 1992.

Ottaviani, Jim. *Wire Mothers: Harry Harlow and the Science of Love.* Ann Arbor, MI: General Tectronics, 2007.

Oxman, T.E., and D.H. Freeman. "Lack of social participation or religious strength and comfort as risk factors for death after cardiac surgery in the elderly." *Psychosomatic Medicine,* 1995, 37, 5–15.

Pennebaker, J.W. *Opening Up: The Healing Power of Confiding in Others.* New York: William Morrow, 1990.

Pollack, John. "See the analogies, change the world." *The Wall Street Journal,* November 8, 2014, C3.

Reichheld, Frederick. "Lead for loyalty." *Harvard Business Review,* August 2001, 76–84.

Riley, Pat. *The Winner Within.* New York: Penguin, 1994.

Rosenbaum, Mark. "Restaurants serve social sustenance." *Journal of Social Research,* 9 (1): (2006): 59–72.

Rosenthal, Robert, and Lenore Jacobsen. *Pygmalion in the Classroom: Teacher Expectations and Pupils Intellectual Development.* New York: Crown, 2003.

Russek, L.G., and G.E. Schwartz. "Perceptions of parental caring predict health status in mid-life: a 35-year follow-up of the Harvard Mastery of Stress Study." *Psychosomatic Medicine,* 1997, 59 (2), 144–149.

Sayles, L.R. *The Working Leader: The Triumph of High Performance Over Conventional Management Principles.* New York: McGraw-Hill, 1993.

Schultz, Howard. "I could smell things were wrong." *Business Week,* April 4, 2011, 102.

Seligman, Martin. *Learned Optimism.* New York: Knopf Doubleday, 2006.

Seyle, Hans. *The Stress of Life, Revised Edition*. New York: McGraw-Hill Education, 1978.

Shurkin, Joel. *Terman's Kids: The Groundbreaking Study of How the Gifted Grow Up*. New York: Little, Brown & Co, 1992.

Sosa, R., et al. "The Effect of a Supportive Companion on Perinatal Problems, Length of Labor, and Mother-Infant Interactions." *New England Journal of Medicine*, 1980, 303, (11).

Surowieki, James. "All together now." *The New Yorker*, April 8, 2005, 26.

Suzuki, Shunryu. *Zen Mind, Beginner's Mind*. Boston: Shambhala Publications, 2011.

Taylor, Shelley. *The Tending Instinct*. New York: Henry Holt & Company, 2002.

Thomas, C.B., and K.R. Duszynski. "Closeness to parents and the family constellation in a prospective study of five disease states: suicide, mental illness, malignant tumor, hypertension and heart disease." *John Hopkins Medical Journal*, 1973, 134, 251.

Valente, Judith. "United crew credits special training for helping to save plane during crisis." *The Wall Street Journal*, March 3, 1989, 1.

Vaillant, George. *Triumphs of Experience: The Men of the Harvard Grant Study*. Cambridge: Harvard University Press, 2012.

Van Dierendonck, Dirk, Wilmar Schaufeli, and Bram Buunk. "Burnout and inequity among human service professionals: A longitudinal study." *Journal of Occupational Health Psychology*, 1992, 22,173–189.

Waber, Ben, Jennifer Magnolfi, and Greg Lindsay. "Workspaces that move people." *Harvard Business Review*, October 2014, 69–77.

Weick, Karl. *Managing the Unexpected*. New York: Wiley, 2007.

Weiss, Jeff, and Jonathan Hughes. "Want collaboration? Accept-and-Actively Manage Conflict." *Harvard Business Review*, March 2005, 93–101.

Werner, Emmy, and Ruth Smith. *Overcoming the Odds: High-Risk Children from Birth to Adulthood*. Ithaca: Cornell University Press, 1992.

Williams, Redford. *Anger Kills*. New York: Harper Collins, 1998.

Wooden, John, and Steve Jamison. *Wooden on Leadership*. New York: McGraw-Hill, 2005.

Wozniak, Steve. *iWoz: Computer Geek to Cult Icon*. New York: W.W. Norton, 2006.

INDEX

ABOUT THE AUTHORS

Bob Maurer is a clinical psychologist on the faculty of the UCLA and the University of Washington School of Medicine. He is also the Director of Behavioral Science for the Family Medicine Residency in Spokane, Washington. He has served as a consultant to Walt Disney Studios, the U.S. Navy and Air Force, Four Seasons Hotels, and Habitat for Humanity. His book on creativity and change, *One Small Step Can Change Your Life*, is available in 16 languages. His lectures and workshops provide audiences with tools for creating and sustaining excellence in health, relationships, and career. Dr. Maurer can be contacted at *www.scienceofexcellence.com*.

Michelle Gifford, MA, CCC-SLP, is a clinical speech language pathologist in private practice and a consultant-educator for families and teams, developing programs of excellence on behalf of children with special needs. She has served as an adjunct faculty member at Eastern Washington University and Washington State University's graduate school programs in communication disorders. Michelle lives in Nine Mile Falls, WA with her husband and youngest son.